Intuition

Discover the Inner Workings of Our World - Book 1

Zamm Zamudio

Zammtopia Publishing

Line Editor: Alana Garrigues
Cover Designer: Nathaniel Dasco
Book Formatter: Z. Z. Henkel

Published in 2018 in New Zealand by
Zammtopia Publishing
Suite 3 Level 8, Munro Benge House
104 The Terrace, Wellington 6011
Email: zammtopia@gmail.com
www.zammtopia.com

ISBN 978-0-473-41828-1 (Kindle Edition)
ISBN 978-0-473-41827-4 (Print Edition)

Disclaimer:

This book includes a discussion of diet and exercise, as well as mental illness. These are meant to illustrate the relationship between health and wellness and a person's ability to tap into intuition.

The examples are based on personal experience and widely published resources on nutrition.

They are not meant to diagnose or treat illness or to assess the reader's health.

Please consult your medical professional before making any changes to diet or exercise, or if you think you may be experiencing an illness.

To Andy, Nigel, Nicole, Brent, Joseph

and

Nanay, Tatay, Lola Mommy,
Mama and Daddy-O

Intuition

Contents

Introduction	1
Part 1: Overview	5
Chapter 1 Intuition?	6
What's in a Word?	9
Intuition at Work	10
Intuition Network	12
Part 2: The Inner Workings of Intuition	16
Chapter 2 Intuiting	17
Chapter 3 Zamm's Intuition Quadrants	26
ZIQ1 - The Intuition Process	27
Perception	28
Instinct	33
Insight	37
Intuition	42
ZIQ2 - The Fundamental Factors of Intuiton	46
Genetics	49
Epigenetics	53
Physiology	57
The Heroes of Mt. Everest	63

Double D: Design and Discipline   64

The Colour of Music   67

Environment   69

Personal Environment   70

Social Environment   72

The Heart and the Hearth   73

Culture   74

The Gist of the Matter   76

Voices   80

Experiences and Development   82

Memory, Learning and Identity   89

Part 3: The Practicalities of Intuition   96

Chapter 4   The Dependencies of Intuition   97

Know Thyself   98

Health and Lifestyle   101

Diet and Essential Nutrients   102

Brain   104

Eyes   106

Ears   109

Smell and Taste   112

The Nose that Knows   113

Buddy Buds   115

Skin and Touch   117

Touch of Hope   120

Muscles and Joints   121

Blood Vessels   122

Nutrition Guide 122

Exercise 134

Sleep 138

Part 4: Developing Intuition 145

Chapter 5   Thinking Methods 146

Timing is Everything 146

Memory and Imagination 149

The Right Way to Worry 150

The Triunity Approach 153

Positive + Negative = Workable Area 155

Past + Future = Present 158

Triple Perspective = Me + S/He/They = Us 161

Multidirectional, Multidimensional Thinking 164

Understanding and Appreciating Diversity 165

The Centre 167

Removing the Blinders 170

Peripheral Vision and Sidelights 175

Chapter 6   Intuition Tools 179

Diary or Journal 179

Brainwave Frequencies and Entrainment 182

Brainwaves 183

Brainwave Entrainment 187

Nature 189

Meditation 191

Dreams 193

Lucid Dreaming 197

Dream Interpretation 199

The Tarot 201

The Deck 203

Reflection 204

Part 5: Fantastical Intuition 207

Chapter 7   Back to The Beginning 208

Appendix :   Sources arranged per chapter
and in alphabetical order 214

Acknowledgements 245

Introduction

When I think of intuition, I'm reminded of the song 'All of Me', written by Gerald Marks and Seymour Simons in 1931, and originally sung by Ruth Etting. Many artists have covered it over the years.

All of me
Why not take all of me
Can't you see
I'm no good without you

Why does the song make me think of intuition? It is because a deeper appreciation of intuition requires every bit of our being — mind and body working together.

I wrote this book in an attempt to 'reverse engineer', or deconstruct, the required processes and elements that form intuition. As a consequence, I realised that intuition needs us in our entirety. The only time we will ever be ready for its amazing influence in our lives is once we have a deeper understanding of *who*, *what* and *how* we are as people.

Although this is not an academic book, I did extensive research to find relevant information to support the ideas I present to you. I hope that you will find them stimulating enough to jump-start your own path to understanding — and living each day — the invaluable guidance of intuition. I further hope it expands your perspective and starts you off on your own journey of curiosity, openness, discovery, and exploring your own *what-ifs*.

I share my personal experiences with you to highlight the scientific studies and ideas presented. I encourage you to relate both the studies and my experiences to your own circumstances for further reflection.

The first part of the book will give you a general idea of what intuition is and how people use and access it. You will see that it is omnipresent, manifested across time and cultures as expertise, particularly by successful people in their chosen fields.

The second part of the book gets into the processes and elements that make intuition work ordinarily and extraordinarily. I highlight the five senses and our physiological processes, the importance of genetic inheritance, and the personal experiences critical to intuition. By recognising all these, I hope that you become more appreciative of your incredible mind and body.

The third part is about the practicalities of intuition, highlighting self-care. This part might be challenging if you're easily distracted, but it is imperative that you read it, and not skim it or skip over it. There is no shortcut to self-care. We should, at the very least, know its fundamentals. Our health directly impacts and reflects our ability to intuit. I do not present you with a 'quick fix' guide to intuition because it does not work that way. Intuition and self-care take significant time and effort, and I believe that your health and mind are worth it.

You will see why self-care must be intertwined with daily life, from diet to activities, in order to support your purpose and continuously develop a better and deeper understanding of yourself. So do read on.

After learning the basics of self-care, the fourth part of the book shifts focus to brain training. You will learn a variety of thinking methods and tools to boost intuition.

— The thinking methods and tools are easy and straightforward. You will not have any excuse to practice. Practice leads to mastery. The tools in this book should give you enough information to form your own idea of a regimen or structure that works for you.

— A discussion on the five different types of brainwaves provides you with an idea of how brain entrainment works and will help you identify whether there are any brainwaves you would like to explore further. Brain entrainment can be used for better focus, for total relaxation, or to explore your higher consciousness, among other things.

— Dream interpretation, lucid dreaming, and Tarot are excellent tools to deepen awareness of your thought processes, your self-perception, your experiences, and the world around you. They are rife with opportunity for self-reflection.

The fifth and final part of the book is about fantastical intuition. It is the sort of intuition that works in a bewildering way because its fantastical manifestations are difficult to fathom and deconstruct. It is largely unstudied because we do not have the tools to measure it. I cannot yet tell you how to bring about fantastical intuition, but I can tell you that it exists, and share my story. I hope that in the future we will have the resources to understand it.

In the meantime, I share how many forms of intuition are easily accessible through self-care and dedication to awareness.

I have included an appendix with my research sources to articles and additional information, arranged by chapter and in alphabetical order, with webpage links as available, so that it will be easier for you to access them in case you want to read more about the topics presented.

I remain authentic throughout the book about my thoughts, and I share my experiences with the intention of making it easier for you to relate my stories to your own unique elements of intuition.

As you read through this book, study the basis and practicalities of intuition, and get to know my journey, I expect you'll examine your own memories and experiences, perhaps relating to some of my own, and the scientific studies I present.

Along the way, I hope that you will find your authentic self as a consequence.

Part 1: Overview

Chapter 1   Intuition?

A few years back, I awoke, startled, from a 'vision and feeling' of being punched and beaten by several men. More of an 'experience' than a dream, I remember begging them to stop while trying to protect my face. I tried to block their punches with my arms, but they just kept hitting me. It was horrible and very scary. As soon as I snapped out of my dreamlike state and regained full consciousness, I thought of my brother, and a terrible feeling came over me. I just knew something was very wrong.

I messaged my uncle, who was semi-looking-after my brother back in the Philippines. My brother has mental and physical disabilities, yet he is stubborn, opinionated and dislikes any representation of an authority figure. For these reasons, he loves living on his own in the province. It affords him the freedom to go wherever he wants to go and do whatever he wants to do. My uncle assured me that he would give me an update as soon as he had one.

It took a few days for my uncle to get back to me. When he did, my fear was confirmed. My brother had been beaten up and would need proper medical care, only available in the city. What my uncle told me reinforced my 'vision and feeling' as what my brother had experienced — getting beaten up by three men — around the same time I had that horrible knowing. Fortunately, my uncle agreed to take care of him until he was robust and back to his old stubborn self. Not surprisingly, my brother returned to the province as soon as he was well.

In late 2016, another dreadful 'knowing' about my brother came to me, this time that he was gravely ill. I had a nagging feeling in my heart that lasted for several days and wouldn't go away, so I reached out via social media to ask if anyone in the province had seen him lately. I found out later through my uncle that my brother was indeed almost dying.

We — my uncle, my aunts, some concerned people and myself — once again rallied to help my brother bounce back to health and life. As everyone anticipated, as soon as he got his strength back, no amount of persuasion from any of us could stop him from going back to the independent lifestyle he chooses. We were left only with the hope that he would stay well for a very long time.

These two incidents illustrate a profound connection between my brother and myself. I'm not at all surprised since it's just the two of us now. Our parents passed away a long time ago. The connection between us is what I consider an example of what I call 'fantastical intuition'. When it comes to my brother, I just *know* without knowing *how* I know.

Not every manifestation or process of intuition is fantastical. We practice intuition to varying degrees in our daily life, and that is what I wanted to more fully understand, explore, and explain when I set out to write this book. I hope to share with you a practical appreciation and approach to developing and strengthening your intuition in the process.

I facilitate workshops and teach classes about intuition, dreams and the Tarot. When I ask my students their definition of intuition, I always get the same three answers, and they generally come up in the same order. The first is 'gut feeling'. The second focuses on one's inner voice. And finally, the third, which is harder to explain — that fantastical and superpower-like form of intuition, often attributed to the mysteries of life which focus on the unseen, veiled with magick or spirituality.

On the surface, the first two thoughts about intuition are easy to grasp, and yet many of us doubt or overrule gut feelings and our inner voice. I'm saddened that often when intuition and the third school of thought — the fantastical version — are associated, people choose not to dig deeper. It feels lazy to me to accept fantastical intuition at face value, not to peel back the layers of this potentially life-changing ability. Extra effort is required, but I expect that the scientific discoveries will make the research worthwhile. Intuition is not an alien concept. We all have it, but we often drown it out with our very human rigidness for logic, our lack of imagination, and distractions from the constant bombardment of noise from the world around us.

What's in a Word?

To understand intuition, let's first deconstruct the processes and factors involved in its development, starting with its most common definitions.

Oxford Living Dictionary defines *intuition* as 'the ability to understand something instinctively, without the need for conscious reasoning', whereas *Cambridge Dictionary* defines it as '(knowledge from) an ability to understand or know something immediately based on feelings rather than facts'.

The word *intuition* has its origin in Latin. It began as *intueri*, meaning 'look at, consider', which evolved in late Latin into *intuitio*, and eventually became *intuition* in Middle English around the mid-fifteenth century.

Intuition is recognised as powerful across industries.

Eugene Sadler-Smith, leading intuition researcher and Professor of Organizational Behavior at Surrey Business School, says intuition denotes 'spiritual insight or direct spiritual communication'. Timothy R Walker, Associate Professor of History at UMass Dartmouth and author of *Elemental Wisdom in Teacher Training* defines intuition as follows: 'to look at attentively with astonishment or admiration, also to gaze and to contemplate or to pay close attention'.

I combine the definitions and origin of the word to describe intuition as an awareness of something extraordinary which elicits astonishment and admiration. It is a shift in focus encouraging reflection and requiring a degree of involvement. It is spiritual insight and direct spiritual communication that transcends the physical world. Its spiritual aspect operates without limitations and physical boundaries and is instantaneous.

When we take this holistic view of intuition, it sounds like the fantastical definition I use to sum up my experiences with my brother. Our communication transcends space and time, and I can only explain it as simply and aptly as 'spiritual'.

Perhaps you have had a similar experience with fantastical intuition?

Keep those personal experiences and anecdotes in mind as we continue to deconstruct and understand the inner workings of intuition. I will share my personal stories of intuition as well, connecting them to expert research and studies.

Intuition at Work

At the time this book went to press, an internet search for 'studies on intuition' resulted in 51,000,000 results in 0.48 seconds. Narrowing it down to scholarly articles revealed 730,000 results in 0.02 seconds. Those figures are as mind-boggling as the many secrets of intuition we have yet to uncover.

Intuition is natural and omnipresent. We often hear stories of women's intuition, or of professionals who 'follow their gut' to make life-saving or life-changing decisions. They're not tall tales. These stories of intuition are backed by solid research.

In 1987, H Fischbein released *Intuition in Science and Mathematics*, a book which asserted that intuition remains the ultimate reliable source of absolute truths in both science and mathematics.

San Diego State University Professor of Economics Roger Frantz, author of *Two Minds: Intuition and Analysis in the History of Economic Thought,* wrote that intuition was vital in guiding many of the greatest minds in history towards their notable discoveries, inventions, innovations, and breakthroughs. Among those guided: Mathematician Bernhard Riemann for his work on prime numbers, Theoretical Physicist Albert Einstein and his theories of relativity, Medical Researcher Jonas Salk in the development of the polio vaccine, and Geneticists Linus Pauling and James Watson, credited with discovering DNA structure.

Imagine a world without any of those discoveries. It's almost impossible.

Asta Raami, in her doctoral dissertation 'Intuition Unleashed', referenced studies showing many Nobel laureates use intuition as their primary thinking mode for discoveries. Throughout the dissertation, Raami presents: how intuition guides logic and complements reasoning; and why practice is necessary to develop intuition until it becomes reliable and second nature.

I read an interesting article in *Investopedia* by Ian Harvey titled 'Decision-Making Methods: Informed, Uninformed, Intuitive'. He wrote about how intuitive veteran traders make seemingly odd and risky choices that pay off. They use intuition to master pattern recognition, resulting in the best chances at making a killing in the stock market. Practice and experience are crucial to getting into this kind of decision-making zone, in which the trader has become so adept at seeing the patterns that it is easier and quicker to make a decision, rather than try to explain the steps taken leading to it.

And then there's the study 'Clinical Intuition in Family Medicine: More than First Impressions' by Dr Olga Kostopoulou and PhD Candidate Amanda Woolley, about family physicians in London who occasionally practise intuition in diagnosing their patients. Kostopoulou and Woolley found that intuitive decision-making, though in conflict with a more rational explanation, was consistently found to lead to better performance than analytic deliberation.

Intuition Network

Intuition helps me every day, even in dilemmas I would consider insignificant — such as finding parking. For years, I've been able to tap into details about when and where my friends and family and I could find parking, down to how many minutes we would have to wait, and even which car would leave the soonest. My friends probably thought I was nuts at first (I explained it, jokingly, by telling them that I have 'my invisible friends' who show me where to park), but soon enough they believed. They would wait patiently, and we always found parking exactly as I had instructed. My youngest adult son asked me once if I hear voices during these times to which I answered, 'No!'

There are no voices. Just this sense of 'knowing'.

His question made me think though, and the only explanation that made sense to me was that, perhaps, I see subtle patterns. I've reflected on it quite a lot, and I don't recall anything specific that would point me to the right car, much less indicate how much time we would have to wait. It defies logic and common sense. Perhaps my car parking senses fall within the family of fantastical intuition. Regardless of how much I think about it and try to explain it, I can't. I just know it works.

A student of mine once told me that he trusts his intuition to choose walking routes. He is mindful and feels for 'better vibes' to guide him to work, the grocery store, anyplace he goes. It might sound bizarre, even trivial, but he feels his intuition leads him to the fastest, safest and most pleasant path.

Other students 'feel the vibes' (trust their intuition) when interacting with others. They interpret vibes visually as either red or green flags, or sometimes the 'heebie-jeebies', a warning system that something is amiss, even before it becomes apparent.

I believe that intuition arises in people who are open to it, flexible, and possess the ability to transcend logic or that which is visible.

Openness gives us the necessary humility to accept, or at least entertain, the concept that our inability to explain certain things does not render them false or unreal. When we are open, we have freedom, courage and creativity — not just to explore uncharted territories where intuition may lead, but also to move beyond limits.

Each of us is naturally intuitive, partly because we are all connected and have access to a 'collective consciousness or unconsciousness', akin to an intuition network. At the University of Chicago, Anna Piepmeyer culled through dozens of articles and studies on the subject to define *collective consciousness* as 'an internal knowing known by all'.

I believe that the intuition network could be made up of the collective representations of universal human themes — love, happiness, freedom, hope, fear, desire, our need to procreate, to leave a legacy, and a longing to connect. There is also a universal human need and urgency to ponder existential questions and to seek solutions to problems, including those that could be a threat to our existence, such as disease.

There is a remarkable concept called *multiple independent discovery*, which supports my concept of an intuition network. In *multiple independent discovery,* two or more people living on opposite ends of the world — complete strangers — come up with the same invention or scientific discovery at the same time.

There are several well-known examples, including Charles Darwin and Alfred Russel Wallace, who discovered the theory of the evolution of the species, and Isaac Newton and Gottfried Wilhelm Leibniz, who formulated calculus. In fact, it is not unusual to hear of Nobel laureates sharing recognition for having made the same discoveries independently. As recently as 2015, Takaaki Kajita of Japan and Arthur B. McDonald of Canada shared the Nobel Prize in Physics when each proved — simultaneously and individually — that neutrinos have mass.

Part 2: The Inner Workings of Intuition

Chapter 2   Intuiting

We often perceive intuition as mystical, magical or fantastical because it holds far-reaching answers to the inner workings of our world. And yes, it can be all of that, but it is also practical, experiential and scientific. I dream that one day we will be able to run a scientific study on intuition, researching thousands, tens of thousands, even a million participants over a period of many years, to gain a much more comprehensive picture and understanding of what it is and how it works as a group and as individuals.

At the individual level, humans experience intuition uniquely and in a very personal way. We call on it, listen to it, use it, with widely varied frequency and intensity. Some of us rely on practical intuition to guide us every day, while others call on intuition only on occasion, say to keep out of harm's way (*gut feeling or fantastical intuition*) or make a big life decision (*inner voice*).

Our own experiences with intuition are generally related to our understanding of and resonance with it.

We are all different. We see things differently. The things I appreciate and value may not be the things you appreciate and value. Our beliefs might conflict. And even if we agree on much, we perceive the world differently. For example, if you and I stood in the same room, if we witnessed the same event, we would perceive it and remember it distinctly. We would experience it differently.

Figure 1. Meet Jazz, our baby spuggler (spooner, snuggler, and cuddler). She is the youngest in the family.

If a stranger, who sees cats as mere pets and nothing more, were to visit our home and witness how I interact with our fur baby Jazz, our 13-year-old cat (see Figure 1), they might perceive and remember me as a kooky cat lady. But I regard what I'm doing as natural.

Treating Jazz as the youngest member of our family, taking care of her in a manner that is no less attentive than I would take care of a human child, letting her sleep beside me and share my pillow, might seem a bit extreme to others. For me, it is how I love her and care for her. It's intuitive — I don't even have to think about it. All I want, all that my family wants, is to make her feel safe and cherished. It rings especially true for me. After all, I am her human mother, and she is very attached to me and relates to me in that role.

Our *perception* is different. The way we experience the world around us and how we process thoughts influence our memories. That is what makes it challenging to measure and control intuition in a scientific environment, and it may require a great deal of technological advancement, new scientific knowledge, and a leap of faith to overcome such challenges.

Intuition is a leap from logic and reasoning, yet the ability to 'know without knowing how we know' resonates as truth and fact, undoubtedly with its own set of triggers and correlations.

Perhaps we can better appreciate how intuition works in the background by identifying: the processes or steps we use to gather and interpret information; what makes those processes unique for each person; and which factors influence the processes.

How do we gather and interpret information?

We receive information through our senses and interpret it by means of *perception*. The way we perceive ourselves and the world around us influences our thoughts, emotions, and behaviours. And our thoughts, emotions, and behaviours influence our perception. It works both ways. Each directly impacts our decision-making abilities, which, naturally, fall anywhere on the spectrum of brilliant and stupid.

When we perceive danger or a threat, and we need to act instantaneously, *instinct* kicks in.

Instinct is the master of self-preservation. It is primal.

Once we've had time for reflection, instinct leads to *insight*. Insight tells us more than that which is visible on the surface. It is complex. When we reflect on our own perceptions and instinctual responses, we recognise critical highlights and patterns. Continuous exposure to similar situations — as well as teaching or mentoring others, or trying to break free from detrimental patterns that keep repeating themselves in our lives — provides excellent opportunities to practice insight, and <u>in</u> time leads to mastery.

Mastery means that any given task or process becomes natural, effortless, and quicker to perform.

Mastering insight means we no longer need time to reflect because we are now capable of 'instant insight', or *intuition*. At this point, *perception* can trigger *intuition*.

Jonas Salk said that intuition might be a continuation or extension of 'natural' processes, such as instinct. We first sense and then we reason why. Roger Frantz described intuition as an innate quality that can be developed and cultivated to achieve a degree of competency. Both examples bring to mind the Johari window and the Four Stages of Learning.

The Johari window, created by psychologists Joseph Luft and Harrington Ingham, is a technique for better understanding our relationships with ourselves and with others. Four quadrants represent degrees of self-awareness and how others relate to us, which in turn impacts our behaviour, attitudes, emotions, skills, and perspectives.

The four quadrants are:

(1) open: what we know about ourselves and what others know about us;

(2) hidden: what we know about ourselves that others do not know about us;

(3) blind spot: what we don't know about ourselves that others do; and

(4) unknown: what we and others don't know about ourselves.

	Known to self	Unknown to self
Known to others	Open	Blind Spot
Unknown to others	Hidden	Unknown

Figure 2. The Johari Window

The Johari window (*see Figure 2*) is most effective in a trusting environment because it involves opening up to others so that they may better understand or know us. Through the vulnerability that comes with being 'known', we expand our own understanding of the self. We learn how others perceive us through constructive feedback, intended and used for personal development and improved teamwork.

For example, some of us might be in the habit of mindlessly doing something we enjoy, like singing or dancing. One day, while we're singing or dancing like no one's watching, someone we love or respect catches us in action and compliments us on how fantastic we are. Without that encouragement, without sharing that moment of mindless reverie with another, even unintentionally, it may never have occurred to us that we possess a natural talent that we'd like to pursue further. But once our talent is realised through the eyes of another, we can choose to practise, gain confidence, maybe even join and win contests. That external recognition of our mindless habit will have opened opportunities that changed our lives for the best. Looking back at the Johari window, we've just awakened to a blind spot and benefited from it.

The Four Stages of Competence, developed by Noel Burch in 1970 for his employer Gordon Training International, describe the four stages of learning any new skill.

(1) We are initially unaware of how little we know.

(2) Once we recognise that which we do not know,

(3) we decide to learn and begin to use our new skill, with effort.

(4) Eventually, the skill becomes 'second nature' and requires no conscious thinking to perform. At this stage, it is possible to teach the skill.

Applying the Johari window method, the Four Stages of Competence would look like this:

COMPETENCE

<table>
<tr><td rowspan="2" style="writing-mode: vertical-rl">CONSCIOUSNESS</td><td>Conscious
Incompetent

2</td><td>Conscious
Competent

3</td></tr>
<tr><td>1
Unconscious
Incompetent</td><td>4
Unconscious
Competent</td></tr>
</table>

Figure 3. The Four Stages of Competence in a Johari Window

Have you ever been lost in thought while driving, only to realise you've arrived at your destination, not entirely aware of how it happened? A bit worrisome, right? I've done it too. It's a little scary to realise that we go on autopilot more often than we would like to admit. It makes me think of *Click,* the bittersweet Adam Sandler movie featuring a man who goes through life on autopilot, missing out not only on the mundane, but what's important as well.

Attaining a skill level of *unconscious competence* is excellent, but it's always best to be aware. Awareness — often referred to as mindfulness — is essential so that we remember the process. Every time we commit a process or experience to memory, we add to our intuition bank.

Chapter 3 Zamm's Intuition Quadrants

The Johari window inspired me to create my own tables, each with four quadrants, holding the elements that I consider the inner workings of intuition. The elements function independently, progressively, and even simultaneously.

I call them Zamm's Intuition Quadrants 1 & 2 (ZIQ1 & ZIQ2).

ZIQ1 illustrates the *Intuition Process,* in which:

(1) *perception* triggers

(2) *instinct* and/or

(3) *insight,* and eventually leads to

(4) *intuition*.

Memory glues the whole process together and influences mastery, which is discussed in ZIQ2. At the highest level of mastery, in the moment *perception* triggers *intuition*, *intuition* can be used to alter *perception*. *(See Figure 4, ZIQ1, next page)*

ZIQ2 illustrates the *Fundamental Factors of Intuition,* unique to each of us, that influence the nature and acuity of our intuitiveness. They are:

(1) *inheritance* divided into genetics, epigenetics and physiology;

(2) *environment* divided into personal, social, and cultural;

(3) *experiences and development*; and finally

(4) *memory*, which is responsible for building our repository of lessons and cues, learned and mastered. It is derived from each of the factors listed above, alone and in combination. *(See Figure 7, ZIQ2, page 46.)*

ZIQ1 - The Intuition Process

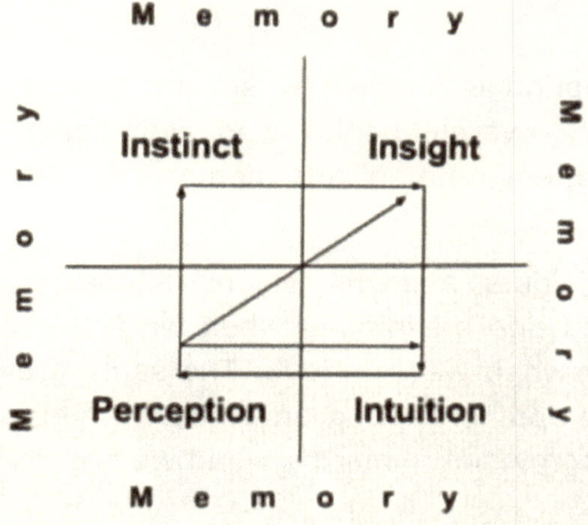

Figure 4. ZIQ1

Perception

Oxford Living Dictionary defines *perception* as 'the ability to see, hear, or become aware of something through the senses', or 'awareness of something through the senses'. It is the act of perceiving. What does it mean to perceive? According to *Online Etymology Dictionary*, the verb 'to perceive' comes from the Latin word *percipere* which literally meant 'obtain, gather, seize entirely, take possession of', but also figuratively meant 'to grasp with the mind, learn, comprehend' — a combination of the roots *per* + *capere* for 'thoroughly' and 'to grasp, take'.

We perceive, or 'take possession of', information primarily by using our five senses — sight, touch, hearing, smell and taste. Some people also tap into a sixth sense linked to acute intuition.

Our perception is shaped by several factors, including physiology, overall health and well-being, personal experience, environment and memory.

Shapes, colours and dimensions appear more vivid, pronounced and meaningful when we feel exceptionally healthy or when we're in love. The same grey day that looks cozy and comforting on a day we feel fulfilled will appear gloomy and menacing when we are sick or sad.

The sounds that we hear — both natural and human-made, in a wide range of tones, pitches, and frequencies (e.g. a love song, lapping waves, birds chirping) — resonate differently during particular moods or stages in life. The voice of the person we love is music to our ears, but when (*if?*) the relationship fails, it sounds annoying.

Smell, whether a scent is fragrant or sickening, has the power to remind us of a particular person or moment in our lives. A familiar scent, such as Nana's perfume, can open a floodgate of memories and emotion in one person, while it has no effect on someone else, beyond a quick whiff of something floral, or sweet. Without memory of a personal connection, it lacks meaning, so the perception is weak.

Those of us who love to eat savour many flavours — sweet, sour, pungent, bitter, spicy. We associate foods with favourite moments, location and people in our lives. But, we know that not all we eat is good for us. Food that tastes so delicious, when consumed excessively, can be detrimental to our health. Once we know that, sugars, salts and fats may start to taste less appealing.

We notice texture, temperature, the relative hardness or softness of things, and that sense of touch drives much of intuition and perception. Most of us seek the warm, gentle, soothing nature of human touch and connection. After all, it is very much a part of intimacy. But for some, intimacy is frightening or unwanted. Touch, perhaps more than any other sense, relates to our sense of safety.

We all create our reality based on perception. When all five senses combine, our perception leads to a more complete view of reality. However:

Not everything we perceive is real.

What may seem real to us doesn't always seem real to a neighbour, a friend, or a stranger. In their book *Perception,* Robert Sekuler and Randolph Blake say that perception is a personal theory of reality, a knowledge-gathering process that defines how we look at the world. I get that! A soldier could be viewed as a saviour by one side, but a destroyer by the other. The leader of a nation can be so polarising that some see them as a problem solver while others see them as the source of the problem.

Have you ever been on one of those 3D rides at an amusement park? Some of my favourites are The Mummy and Harry Potter at Universal Studios Hollywood, and Twilight Zone Tower of Terror (now retired) at Disneyland. Why bring them up now? The rides are designed to trick our senses into feeling, seeing and hearing simulations — things that are not real. They are a perfect illustration that perception is not always real. I am not really battling giant spiders or running away from ghosts, even though my senses of sight and sound tell me that I am. I find these kinds of deceptive immersion stimulating and enjoyable, but others perceive them as frightening.

Perception is very much affected by our natural sensory preferences that dictate how we learn and remember. Some people are visual. Others are tactile-kinesthetic or auditory. And then there are multisensory learners who experience visual, tactile and audible sensory stimulations equally and contemporaneously.

Figure 5. Kitty Chelsea

Meet Kitty Chelsea (*Figure 5*), our first fur baby. She was enjoying the box and having a nap. It might seem at first glance that Kitty Chelsea was using her Jedi superpowers to make it levitate! I promise you it was nothing but the odd placement of the shadow. The box was firmly on the carpet.

Perception can be misleading.

Figure 6. Kat the Cat

Meet Kat (*Figure 6*), our second fur baby. She was a medium-sized cat, but this picture begs to differ. My placement while taking her photo and her pose turned her into a seemingly enormous cat with a small head!

Perception can be inaccurate.

Instinct

Cambridge Dictionary defines *instinct* as 'a natural ability that helps you decide what to do or how to act without thinking', or 'the ability to behave in a particular way that has not been learned'. Once again, we turn to *Online Etymology Dictionary* and find that 'instinct' comes from the fourteenth-century Old French *instinct,* meaning 'a prompting', and from the Latin *instinctus,* meaning 'instigation, impulse, inspiration'.

Part of what perception does is discriminate against threats. When a threat is identified, instinct is the first responder. It is crucial to survival.

Instinct is natural, automatic, instant and spontaneous.

It is a knee-jerk reaction to anything we perceive as harmful to our life, well-being, or whatever we hold dear.

Instinct needs no time for analysis, introspection or reflection. *It doesn't think*.

In the larger scheme of things, instinct is the preserver of the species. Breathing, sex, desire, a mother's love to protect her young (even to death), a baby's ability to suckle from their mother — all are basic instincts doing their job excellently. Instinct doesn't require conscious thought or prior experience to help us survive. It just acts.

And boy, can make us act!

One of my favourite videos of instinct in action features a dad from Indonesia. A security camera captures him working on his motorcycle on a sidewalk or a garage — somewhere blocked off from traffic — when he somehow notices a car speeding towards his children behind him. He stands, turns, wraps his body around them, and tumbles away from danger, using his body as a protective shield around his children. It is amazing to watch his superhero reflexes, strong and determined, yet from a state of calm. I'm convinced it was the adrenaline, fueled by his instinct to save them that gave him the ability and swiftness to do such a feat. Check him out on YouTube. The video is titled 'Superhero Dad Saves His Children with Lightning Fast Response' and posted by Viralhog.

And then there's another video that amazes me. A babycam catches a nine-year-old boy who saved his 11-month-old baby brother by racing across the room to catch him as he rolled over and fell off the side of the changing table, while mom turned her back for just a moment mid-diaper change. The nine-year-old was halfway across the room but responded with lightning speed. In an interview, the older brother said he couldn't even carry the 11-month-old or run that fast, and he had no idea how he was able to do what he did. That video is also on YouTube, titled '10 Heroic Kids Who Came to the Rescue | ABC News Remix', posted by ABC News.

With the exception of those who live in a war zone or some other dangerous place, we do not face grievous threats all the time. Still, we are hardwired to channel instinct as fight or flight. We run away or act aggressively — anchored to the 'shoot first and ask questions later' mindset.

We often find it challenging to transcend survival mode. In the Harvard Business Review article, 'How Hardwired is Human Behavior?', Nigel Nicholson found that in spite of all our scientific, technological and social progress, we are essentially hardwired to act instinctively. He wrote, 'You can take the person out of the Stone Age, evolutionary psychologists content, but you can't take the Stone Age out of the person.'

It's not a bad thing. I find it comforting to know that we still have the same grit and stubbornness to survive as our cavemen (and cavewomen) ancestors. We're hardwired — programmed — to do whatever we can, whenever we can, in the name of safety and survival.

I believe instinct in its highest form is noble and altruistic.

It may occasionally contradict itself concerning self-preservation, but instinct always remains consistent in its goal to preserve life.

We are all familiar with inspiring stories of people risking their lives for others — firefighters who run into a burning building to save people, soldiers who endanger themselves to bring their injured brethren back from the firing line, ordinary men and women who have jumped in front of subway trains to rescue a stranger who fell on the tracks. There are so many incredible stories of selflessness — people who risked their own lives for the safety of strangers and the ones they love, sometimes dying in the process.

In such cases, the instinct for survival supercedes the self. It is designed to save the lives of others, acting as the preserver of the species.

Instinct is powerful because it is so focused on the present that it leaves no room for anything else.

However, it can be short-sighted, and thus unsustainable.

Relying solely on instinct carries a risk of stagnation in our response mechanisms and in our personal development because we will always be doing what is natural.

It is better to take time to reflect on our *perception* and *instinctual impulses*. By shifting our focus beyond the boundaries of the present, we allow room for *insight*. Otherwise, we could miss out on vital information, compromising our judgement and our future.

Insight

Oxford Living Dictionary defines *insight* as 'the capacity to gain an accurate and deep understanding of someone or something. Per *Online Etymology Dictionary*, the term comes from the eleventh-century *innsihht* meaning 'sight with the 'eyes' of the mind, mental vision, understanding from within'. Over time, an interpretation as 'sight into' has evolved to mean 'penetrating understanding into character or hidden nature'.

Psychologically speaking, *Mosby's Medical Dictionary* defines *insight* as 'a type of self-understanding encompassing both intellectual and emotional awareness of the unconscious nature, origin, and mechanisms of one's attitudes, feelings, and behaviour'.

Insight influences my life significantly, especially in my line of work where I use the Tarot as a tool. I have a TripAdvisor page — find me at *Tarot Zamm* in Wellington, New Zealand — and I request feedback after every session to see how my clients felt about their Tarot reading consultation. Amongst the written and verbal feedback I receive, 'insightful' trumps all other descriptors of their sessions and experiences with the Tarot. My clients describe insight in many ways:

— 'enlightening'

— 'provides clarity on a way forward'

— 'provides information to make more sense of a situation'

— 'very useful in showing the various pathways that were possible'

— 'provides excellent solutions to problems'

— 'put concerns into perspective'

— 'giving knowledge'

— 'eye-opening'

— 'makes me think about things in a way I haven't before'

Gaining insight through the Tarot and our conversation gave them a better understanding of themselves and their situations.

Though the process can take time, insight itself sometimes comes suddenly. Such was the case of Archimedes when he discovered fluid displacement, otherwise known as the physical law of buoyancy, causing him to run naked through the streets of Syracuse, screaming 'Eureka! Eureka!'

Respected German Psychologist and Theoretical Linguist Karl Bühler coined sudden insight *Aha-Erlebnis*, or 'Aha Moment' in English. We also know it as an epiphany.

I have had some Aha-Erlebnis moments of my own. One that I remember particularly well occurred during my last year of high school. I was taking calculus, and I loved it — but it wasn't easy. At the beginning of the school term, I would often catch myself with creased eyebrows and an open mouth, scratching my head, not understanding my teacher's lectures. Though some days it seemed hopeless, I did not give up on myself. I kept listening, even when it sounded like gibberish, until one day, suddenly, I had a different perspective. I finally recognised how the pieces of the calculus 'puzzle' fit together. It took a couple of months to get there, but I had arrived at my calculus epiphany! I was no student extraordinaire, but I passed and was happy with my grade.

My experience in calculus was an example of what Drs. Robert Sternberg and Janet Davidson described in their book, *The Nature of Insight*, as a three-process view of insight. The three steps to insight are:

(1) *selective-coding insight*: separate what is important and what is irrelevant;

(2) *selective-comparison insight*: find a connection between acquired knowledge and experience; and

(3) *selective-combination insight*: understand the different components of the problem and put it all together.

In order to learn calculus, I first filtered relevant information, then joined those concepts to the bits and pieces of mathematics I had previously learned and retained, in order to create a better understanding. Finally, I put everything together as a whole to build up my knowledge and confidence.

Unlike *instinct*, which we've already defined as hardwired and requiring little or no thought, *insight* is formed. I've identified two primary keys to insight:

(1) time and a quiet mind, and

(2) the ability to unfocus on the problem.

What do I mean by *time and a quiet mind*? There is no room for clutter, distractions, overthinking, worries or anything else that would prevent the creation of a 'blank canvas' open to insight.

I am in an entirely different headspace when I write compared to when I do Tarot readings.

A Tarot reading requires me to keep my mind clear and empty so that I can communicate what I see in the cards, as articulately as possible, with my clients.

Writing is the exact opposite. My brain needs to handle all the busyness, filter through it, and organise my thoughts into a coherent narrative.

Writing leaves me unreceptive to the Aha-Erlebnis for my clients, yet it leaves me open to my own. I can't just flip the switch on or off. I can't automatically alternate between headspaces. I have to follow the demands of insight by having entirely separate schedules for Tarot readings and my own writing.

When my mind is clear and empty, I can thoroughly focus on my clients. I discern and relay relevant information that may help them navigate their lives and their challenges more efficiently. Keeping the 'blank canvas' in my mind free and clean allows me to stay relaxed and zoned-in.

Which brings me to my second key to insight: *unfocus on the problem*. It may sound counterintuitive but think of your thought process as those Magic Eye books. You have to unfocus to see what's hidden.

I can imagine the moment when Archimedes had his insight. There he was, getting ready to relax in the bath, finally having some time off after racking his brains nonstop. He slowly shifted his focus towards how pleasant the water temperature was. It felt so welcoming that he dipped into the tub. As he sank in, the water rose to make space and accommodate his tired body. Then BOOM! Eureka! Archimedes noticed the water displacement.

Unfocusing on the problem gives us relief, freedom from pressure and stress, and time to allow thoughts, ideas and experiences to sink in. Even a few minutes in an unfocused state of mind are powerful enough to invite insight to reveal itself.

Relaxing attracts insight. Plus, it is good for our well-being. It replenishes our energies and refreshes our mind so that we can be more receptive.

Insight requires a healthy combination of:

- *genuine curiosity,*
- *interest,*
- *openness,*
- and a *belief* that it is always there for the taking.

It works as long as we balance all four elements with *rest* and *mental freshness.*

Intuition

I believe that when *insight* becomes *instinctive*, *intuition* is born.

The great distance and divide between *perception* and *intuition* disappear, and we get from Point A to Point Z, at once.

The best visual I can use to describe the nature and speed of this process comes from *Star Trek*. I relate the instant relationship between perception and intuition to teleportation. Captain James T Kirk would demand, 'Beam me up, Scotty!' And voilà, in a blink of an eye he would arrive at his intended destination.

I imagine intuition transpires when perception 'beams up' information that arrives as instinctive insight. Memory serves as the high-capability teletransporter, reaching the far corners of the mind's universe. It makes sense, right? Or perhaps my visual was triggered by the word 'frontier', used by Kevin Cloninger, author of the article 'Making Intuition Practical: A New Theoretical Framework for Education'.

He wrote, 'Intuition is the last frontier of the mind, since it is an aspect of cognition that knows no boundaries.'

Cloninger wasn't talking about *Star Trek*, but it resonated with me in such a way that connected the two.

Intuition conveys messages through emotions. Although, it is important to note that in 'Emotion and Intuition', Psychology Professors and Authors Annette Bolte, Thomas Goschke and Julius Kuhl wrote that intense negative emotions silence intuition on certain occasions.

Memories of our experiences elicit emotions that come loaded with many lessons learned. The intensity of those emotions, mainly when learning something new, make the memories vivid and unforgettable which is helpful in keeping the lessons close to our heart. Once we have retained the lessons in our intuition bank, reliving the intensity becomes a distraction which is counterproductive to intuition.

Embedded in our memories are cues and patterns, associated sensory stimulations, and triggers that affect our thoughts and decisions. The more clearly we remember, the more naturally we recognise patterns, the stronger our inner voice becomes. It takes a composed mind to be receptive to this process without being drawn into it.

Combining a composed mind with creative imagination leads to our ability to see many potential paths, priorities, surprises and wildcards. This is called foresight. As soon as we are able to imagine and evaluate alternatives as instantaneously as instinct, we gain intuition.

When I read the Tarot for my clients, I do my best to give them insight. The cards that I draw stimulate my mind with pictures of their many possibilities. Intuition helps me focus on a few of the more manageable and achievable options for my client.

The speed at which these images form is instantaneous. I flip the cards, and as soon as I see them, the words flow from my mouth without conscious thought. I let it happen without resistance. I trust in the process and never question it. I have faith that what I say and what I see will translate into valuable information that my clients need.

What's fascinating is that I usually ask my clients to withhold information from me until I finish discussing their open readings. A vast majority of the time, the messages revealed are relevant to their circumstances.

As one client from Australia wrote, 'I was constantly surprised at how I could relate to the information Zamm was providing us with, and I was impressed at the speed and level of intuition that was being articulated. The open reading immediately touched on issues that we were dealing with in our personal lives, which I find incredible. Specific things were mentioned that echoed almost exactly some things that my partner and I had discussed earlier.'

Connection is a vital element of intuition.

I believe it is the key to accessing the intuition network — the repository of universal human themes to which all of us belong, including my clients and myself. By connecting with my clients at deep levels of honesty, compassion and empathy, I get access to the intuition network, revealing to me their greatest hopes and concerns.

Intuition is my pathfinder, as it is for everyone. The difference between me and some readers who may have picked this book on a whim or out of curiosity — those of you just beginning to express an interest in intuition — is that I have had lots of practice, which started when I was a teenager. Now, every reading I do is an opportunity to further develop my intuitive skill beyond its current level of competency.

Intuition, coupled with *creative imagination*, is an invaluable decision-making tool. It enables our mind to be flexible and keen to discern better ways of doing things. It empowers our free will.

Intuition helps us successfully manoeuvre changes. It makes us wiser by enabling us to see the consequences of our decisions, even before we decide what we're going to do. The mastery with which we can successfully manoeuvre change defines our being, represented by the degree of appreciation we have for our experiences.

Now that we have explored ZIQ1, The Intuition Process, from *perception* to *instinct* to *insight* and finally *intuition*, always remembering that intuition is multidirectional and can activate any and all four processes at once, let us move onto ZIQ2, The Fundamental Factors of Intuition.

I identify the four factors as follows:

(1) inheritance,

(2) environment,

(3) experience, and

(4) memory.

Let's take an in-depth look.

ZIQ2 - The Fundamental Factors of Intuiton

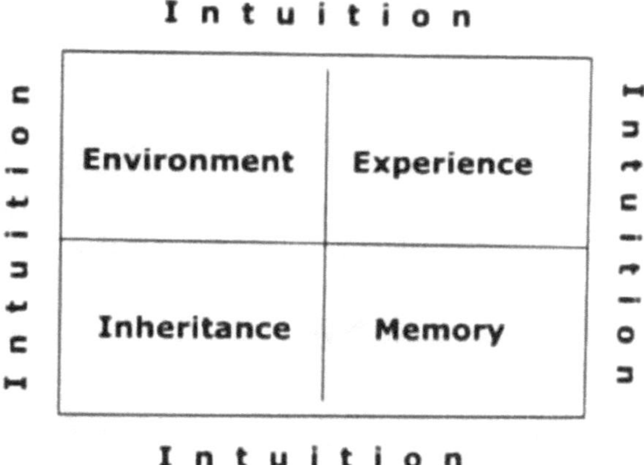

Figure 7. ZIQ2

Inheritance

I was born into a line of 'spiritually sensitive' — better yet, let's call them 'intuitive' — women. I grew up in an extended family setting. My maternal grandmother, Lola Mommy, was the head of the household. She had unyielding intuition which my aunts and uncles funnily called 'radar' (pronounced raah-dar in Filipino). I remember some occasions when her children would think that they had successfully kept 'secrets' from her, only for them to find out that she already knew. Lola Mommy used her intuition exclusively for her family.

I also experienced and benefitted from her intuition. The most memorable incident happened when I took the entrance exams for one of the top science schools in the country. Passing the exams was critical. It was the only way I could graduate from high school for free, as a scholar of the City of Manila. Weeks passed after I took the exams, and still, there had been no news, no mail from the school, of my test results. I was losing hope, almost resigned to the possibility that I had failed.

Lola Mommy noticed this, and with emphatic eyes, she told me, 'Don't worry, you passed. Just ask your Nanay (*my mother*) to go to the campus with you to check.'

I thought she was just trying to calm my nerves and offer me words of encouragement because, after all, she loved her granddaughter. But, as advised, off I went with my Nanay. I remember how nervous and anxious I felt. As if wild butterflies fluttering around in my stomach were trying to escape through my mouth.

We arrived at the school, and lo and behold, Lola Mommy was right! I had passed all the exams, and the rest is history. I went on to graduate from the specialised science high school.

Nanay was highly intuitive as well, but she chose a different path. She helped others find answers to their challenges in life, and on a few occasions searched for missing loved ones. She would say that these 'missing people' often wanted to be found, so it was not hard to connect with them. Often, they had already passed on from our world and wanted closure for those whom they had left behind. She was known for often delivering on her cases, and since she did, some VIPs — including government officials — consulted with her too.

I use the Tarot as my preferred intuition tool. Unlike me, Lola Mommy didn't use anything — just plain old pure intuition. Nanay sometimes complemented her intuition by using ordinary playing cards. Now, I carry the torch. I try my best to help people find their path.

I believe I inherited my intuitiveness, together with my heightened senses of smell, hearing, feeling, and seeing, from both Lola Mommy and Nanay. It's not unusual for me to sense things that others don't. I may be strange in this sense — pun intended, but I'm also very logical and not one to accept things at face value.

Naturally inquisitive, I want answers about how things work. And so, I ponder: Can intuition indeed be passed on within a family, passed down through several generations? If so, how can we sharpen this inheritance? Is it only through our experiences, or are there other ways to strengthen our intuition?

I look at the question of *inheritance* as it relates to intuition through three scientific lenses:

(1) genetics,

(2) epigenetics, and

(3) physiology.

Genetics

Genetics is a favourite part of my research on intuition. I find the concept of how our genetic makeup may contribute to our natural intuitiveness fascinating, and I'm always looking to better understand that relationship.

Stories of 'spiritually sensitive' or highly intuitive women are often similar to my own. When interviewed about their experiences, they'll often say that intuition ran in the family, is passed down from mothers or nanas, sometimes skipping a generation. It would be easy to surmise that, where genetics are involved, intuition comes from our maternal lineage.

And that may be partly true. But imagine my surprise when I learned that in some cases, inheriting a specific gene from our paternal lineage can help women become more socially intuitive.

That finding was established in a study conducted by Professor David Skuse and Dr William Mandy when they were working with girls affected by Turner syndrome. Turner syndrome is a genetic condition where a female has just one X chromosome intact, instead of the usual two. (*Genetics refresher: females are born XX, males are born XY. Turner syndrome only affects females, and one X is either missing or partially missing. It is also known as '45,X' or 'monosomy X', and occurs in 1 in 2,500 newborn girls worldwide.*)

The study focused on 80 girls who have Turner syndrome. Some had difficulties in social settings, particularly at school, while others were doing just fine. Professor Skuse and his team of scientists discovered that the well-adjusted girls had one thing in common: They had inherited their X chromosome from their father, not their mother.

These girls were more socially *intuitive,* better able to function and get along with their peers, friends, and teachers. They were able to cope, adapt, and interpret body language, voice, and conversational tones. Those skills allowed them to sense or become aware of what others might be thinking or feeling, and thus relate better to their peers.

The study got me thinking: What if some highly intuitive women inherit a sort of 'intuitive' X chromosome from their dad? And what if, instead of compensating for the lack of a second X chromosome (as with the girls in Skuse and Mandy's Turner syndrome study), it resulted in overcompensation — an excess of intuition — when paired with their mom's X chromosome?

Taking it a step further: What if a naturally intuitive woman's X chromosome is so particular that it somehow influences her to identify, choose, and mate with a man who possesses a more naturally 'intuitive' X chromosome?

Or what if it's the other way around where dad's 'intuitive' X chromosome is responsible for choosing a female possessing a chromosome with the DNA that can switch on intuition? Is this possible? Could this be how these women became highly intuitive?

Our genes are our blueprint. Within our DNA lie the instructions of our genetic makeup — not just our physical appearance (e.g., eye, hair and skin colours), but behavioural tendencies and predispositions to illnesses.

My Tatay (father) suffered from alcoholism in a culture that didn't accept it as an illness. Instead, it was seen as a weakness of will, a lack of discipline, a mere indulgence. I feel sorry for my dad. He had no support. He struggled and was often misunderstood, frowned upon, and stigmatised. He died very young, at 54. What made him predisposed to this illness? And what made me not? My DNA seems to have responded to his illness with an equal and opposite reaction.

Whereas my father sought alcohol, my body rejects it. I almost died once from drinking a shandy with beer. I got so dehydrated that had I not been taken to the hospital in time, the doctors said I would have surely died. Up to this day, though my tolerance might have improved, I very rarely drink, because I can't. The only thing I can tolerate is a single shot of low-alcohol-content liqueur. Every time I try to be ambitious by having two, I get a nightmarish migraine which is a compelling reminder that I shouldn't dare, or better yet — I should avoid it altogether.

I guess the genes passed down from my Tatay function differently in me, giving me a chance for a better life. A sober life. Whatever genes caused his predisposition to alcohol somehow switched in the opposite direction for me. It's almost as if his genes were intuitive enough to foresee these tendencies and instructed my other genes to react to alcohol in such a way that protects me. Could it be that Tatay's genes chose Nanay, sensing a gene in her that, when combined with his, could turn off my predisposition to alcoholism?

We know that we inherit genetic predispositions to certain diseases such as cancer, diabetes, heart disease, and mental illnesses. Why would a genetic predisposition to intuition be any different?

Epigenetics

What is epigenetics?

A simplified definition of epigenetics is the study of biological processes that switch genes on and off.

Age, the environment, lifestyle, disease, nutrition, stress, relationships — all spur epigenetic change. Epigenetics is responsible for determining how cells differentiate and form into skin cells, liver cells, brain cells, etc. As much as it can build up, epigenetics can also damage the body, resulting in diseases like cancer, autoimmune disorders, and neurological disorders such as Alzheimer and Parkinson's.

Epigenetics reinforces my belief that intuition is at least partly inherited genetically and can be switched on by genes as well as external influences such as the environment or childhood experience.

In my limited understanding of this complex and relatively new scientific field, our genes are like the workers, performing their roles, while epigenetics is the supervisor telling the genes:

> — what organs to make,

> — when to 'level up' or 'shut up' in terms of expressing themselves, and even

> — how to react and evolve when exposed to

>> — changes in the environment,

>> — changes in lifestyle, such as diet and exercise, and

— stressors or inherited genetic memories, both good and bad, from our parents and grandparents, going back at least two generations.

Our *genetic (or epigenetic) inheritance* takes into account the experiences and environmental exposures in our grandparents' lives that led to certain genetic predispositions, which we inherit, along with genetic memory. Interestingly, I'm reminded of a verse I read from the Good Old Book — The Bible — many years ago, which says, 'the sins of the father are passed down to the children (up to the) fourth generation'.

In one recent study, worms subjected to environmental controls were able to retain and pass their experiences down as 'environmental memories' all the way to the fourteenth generation. Think of it. Fourteen generations! That's scary. (If you'd like to learn more about it, search 'Transgenerational Transmission of Environmental Information in C. elegans' by Klosin, Casas, Hidalgo-Carcedo, Vavouri and Lehner.)

In humans, the transgenerational epigenetic effect has been scientifically observed spanning at least two generations. The study 'Transgenerational Effects of Pre-Natal Exposure to the 1944–45 Dutch Famine', by Dr MVE Veenendal, showed that the malnourished environment in utero of those born during the latter part of World War II continued to influence their children's genes. Poor health in utero led to altered body composition and poorer health in their children, particularly for the children of men who had been born malnourished. They had higher rates of obesity than the children of women born between 1944–45.

This means that whatever we experience in utero, whether it be the nutrients we receive or the biology and physiology of our mother, can have a significant long-term effect throughout our adult life, and onto our children.

Researchers continue to study the effects of the Dutch famine, and a recent study by Bas Heijmans and LH Lumey show that the adult children of those undernourished mothers continue to have higher rates of obesity, diabetes, and schizophrenia, their DNA permanently altered.

Epigenetic tags remind genes what they are supposed to be doing. And when epigenetics crosses paths with behavioural science, we see behaviours and affectations passed down from one generation to the next. We may literally inherit our parents' or grandparents' proclivity to intuition, vulnerability to disease, their habits, their fears in the form of a phobia or traumatic response, and even their successes.

Is success in our genes?

Yes, success is shaped by our genes, according to Duke University School of Medicine Professor Dan Belsky and his colleagues. They arrived at the conclusion by cross-referencing socioeconomic data from an ongoing study of 918 people from Dunedin, New Zealand. The study has been tracking the group since they were born, between 1972–73, and has included 12 follow-up appointments to date, ranging in ages from 3 to 38.

Belsky found that a person's 'genetic score' could predict their ability to:

— stay in school,

— be friendly and likeable,

— get along well with others,

— learn a language,

— read and write at an early age

— and have self-control,

all of which contribute to successful adult life. By age 38, those with higher genetic scores had more prestigious occupations, higher incomes, more assets, and were better at managing their finances. Those with high scores tended to outperform even their parents.

Though our genes might give us some advantage from the onset of life, they are not our destiny. We need a suitable nurturing environment to flourish — a harmony of nature and nurture.

The fascinating aspect of epigenetics is that we influence the way our genes work by etching the memory of our environment, for better or worse. Stress, malnutrition and fear can harm our grandchildren's genes. But, by ensuring a significantly supportive and sustaining environment, we can pass positive genetic codes down to our children and their children.

We'll discuss sensible and realistic measures to do this in Chapter 4 when we examine in detail the practicalities of intuition. Once we've set favourable environmental conditions, epigenetics makes it possible to instruct our genes to create or form special physiological functions that make our intuition acute.

Imagine if families and educational systems were designed to encourage and support the development of intuition, through habits formed in daily interactions, starting at a very young age, while the mind is still like a sponge. Home and school are spaces rich in opportunities and abundant with tools.

Epigenetics holds many clues to how intuition is passed down through the generations, particularly when it comes to memories that help form and mould it. I'm sure scientists and experts will find definitive ways to use epigenetics as a form of therapy to strengthen intuition, all in good time.

Physiology

Genetic and epigenetic inheritance significantly impact our final piece in the inheritance of intuition — human physiology.

What is *physiology* and how can it affect intuition?

Of all the definitions I've seen, the University of New South Wales defined it best for a layperson like me. They call *physiology* 'the science of life', continuing, 'physiology is all about what makes our bodies work —

how the organs — including the brain — function, how we grow and develop, how we sustain our bodily functions and what happens to these processes during disease and ageing'. That second part struck me.

If perception is the first step to intuiting, and perception is heavily reliant on physiology, as the sensory systems gather and translate information into something recognisable and understandable, is it possible that the genes of naturally intuitive people created their physiology well-suited for intuiting?

Some animals hear sounds at frequencies that are inaudible to most humans. When we do hear something unusual from a source that is unseen and unexplained, we often say it's from the 'spirit world'. The concept of a spirit world is scary for many, because we don't know much about it, or if it even exists. And yet, we have a term for those who can pick up a range of frequencies from such unknown sources. It's called *clairaudience*, and it is the ability to hear from the spirit world or unknown sources of origin.

According to *Collins English Dictionary*, *clairaudience* is the 'ability to hear sounds beyond the range of normal hearing' or to 'perceive and understand sounds that cannot be heard'.

I'm very open to the possibility that there are genuinely clairaudient people. They may possess a physiology of hearing that picks up a more extensive range of frequencies than the rest of us, from very high to very low, including infrasounds.

What is infrasound? *Merriam-Webster Medical Dictionary* technically defined it as 'a wave phenomenon of the same physical nature as sound but with frequencies below the range of human hearing'.

In his article 'Infrasound — The Frequency of Fear', Roberdo Raval wrote that frequencies lower than 20 Hz, can 'provoke feelings of nervosity, uneasiness and fear… often they occur at places that are held to be haunted'.

Jennifer Oulette, who wrote 'Some "Ghosts" May Be Sound Waves Just Below Human Hearing', said that in private and academic studies (including one at the University of London College) nearly a quarter of people subjected to infrasound described the experience as a presence, being watched, scared, anxious, cold chills down the spine, or pressure on their chest — even if they could not physically hear the sound. Some even hallucinated.

It is apt that infrasound would be called the 'fear frequency'. Some of its known but unseen natural sources come from scary events — avalanches, earthquakes, geomagnetic activity, meteors, ocean waves, severe weather, turbulence, and volcanoes. Physicist Alfred J. Bedard of the National Oceanic and Atmospheric Administration and his team of scientists worked on infrasound sensors to predict natural disasters before they happen.

But not all infrasound sources are known. Perhaps infrasound from unknown sources is a communication line that connects our world to the spirit world, like a spirit frequency for the spirit internet.

What if some people are not only physiologically sensitive to infrasound but also possess an uncommonly wired brain, which allows them to interpret and handle such sensations without getting spooked? Perhaps these are the world's clairaudients, and as a result, they are able to perceive the spirit world. I imagine infrasound frequencies and the sensations they trigger as a form of language easily understood by the clairaudient — not so different from HTML, Javascript or whatever language a programmer knows, understands and uses.

Speaking of frequencies, did you know that humans and cats have a similar range of hearing on the low end of the scale? But cats can hear much higher-pitched sounds, up to 64 kHz, which is 1.6 octaves above the range of a human, and one octave above that of a dog. I guess this is why some perceive cats to be connected to the supernatural. Perhaps because of their acute hearing, they have access to the spirit world.

Moving beyond hearing, what about people who have an acute sense of smell? They possibly have more nose receptors, similar to cats. Cats possess a powerful sense of smell which is 14 times stronger than most humans.

We can also consider 'skin-deep' physiological influences. Humans usually have five million sensory skin receptors that send electrical impulses to the neurons, and relay electrochemical impulses. What if naturally intuitive people have many more?

Is it possible that highly intuitive people, those with a sixth sense or exceptionally in tune with all thirty-three senses put forth by University of Glasgow Psychology Professor Steve Draper, are distinguishing slight changes in their environment (*exteroception*) and inside their bodies (*interoception*) which influence their perception?

What if hypersensitivity to physiological functions inform more precise, focused and information-rich cognitive processes? And what if that enables such people to jump straight to intuition, skipping some of the processes involved in ZIQ1? They could go from perception to instinct to insight at lightning speed.

I have an odd quirk about earthquakes. I usually feel dizzy for several days before one happens. However, I often feel dizzy anyway. So it doesn't mean that when I get dizzy, there'll be an earthquake, even though I do get dizzy before it happens. It's tricky, isn't it? Tell me about it!

It's possible that I'm sensitive to a particular wave emitted before an earthquake, similar to dogs, rats, centipedes, and other animals said to change their behaviour hours to weeks before a seismic event. There are two types of seismic energy. According to Michigan Technological University, body waves travel inside the earth and release the first seismic energy. The sound of body waves is what causes some dogs to bark before an earthquake is felt, though it is not heard by most humans. Surface waves travel through the earth's crust after body waves and are responsible for most earthquake damage.

Since my dizziness can go on for days before an earthquake, I'm not sure which wave I sense. Could there be another form of seismic energy besides the two, one that happens even earlier than a body wave?

Regardless, I think my dizziness is a form of *exteroception*, which means I'm sensitive to stimuli originating outside of my body. It may be one of the reasons I am intuitive. I perceive external sensations more deeply than most. That doesn't mean I can reliably predict an earthquake! My perception can't make that leap to intuition ahead of time. It's only in retrospect that I recognise the sign.

Whenever I feel the blood rushing to my face, I take my blood pressure. The result is often an elevated reading. Sometimes I feel my heartbeat around my neck or temple areas, and hear it in my ears. These are forms of *interoception*, meaning sensitivity to stimuli originating inside of the body.

Exteroception and *interoception* are examples of physiological functions that affect perception and intuitive abilities.

Some well-known people have been the subject of scientific studies because they manifest some form of physiological (genetic, cellular, physical) superabilities. Let's start with the Sherpas.

The Heroes of Mt. Everest

The Sherpas are remarkable people. They have actively supported every known Mt. Everest conquest. The first people ever confirmed to reach the summit were Sherpa Tenzing Norgay and Sir Edmund Hillary of New Zealand. Together, in May 1953, they climbed and conquered the tallest mountain in the world. *Time Magazine* named both to their '100 Most Influential People of the Twentieth Century' list.

The Sherpas are well adapted to function efficiently and expend large amounts of energy at high altitudes. They remind me of ants when I think of their incredible strength. As porters for climbers attempting to reach the summit, they carry towering expedition packs that weigh more than they do. It is not unusual for a 125-pound Sherpa to carry a 150-pound load on their back — and sometimes strapped on their foreheads! Let us not forget that the air becomes thinner the higher the altitude gets. Just like the Energiser Bunny, they just keep going and going, up and down the mountain, every time.

They are so astounding that genetic and physiological studies have been done to understand their superhuman ability and adaptability to such gruelling conditions. Xtreme Everest Co-Founder Dr Denny Levett, along with her colleagues, conducted one pioneering study showing that the Sherpas' mitochondria were much more efficient at harnessing oxygen.

The mitochondria are in nearly all cells of our body. *Biology Dictionary* calls them 'the powerhouse of the cell' because they generate 90% of the energy needed to support life and organ function. We get sick (and could die) when they malfunction.

At sea level, a normal human being's blood is 98-99% saturated with oxygen. It drops to a low of 40% on the summit of Mt. Everest. But Sherpas' bodies can carry oxygen through even the smallest blood vessel in a process called microcirculation. They function exceptionally well at high altitudes because the oxygen can reach muscles, tissues and organs efficiently, giving them superhuman stamina.

This adaptation took hundreds of years, according to another study by Dr Edward T Gilbert-Kawai and his colleagues. They think the process began in the early to mid-sixteenth century when the Sherpas migrated from the Kham region of eastern Tibet to Nepal, where they now live. Continuous exposure to high altitudes, spanning generations, has epigenetically triggered the Sherpas' mitochondrial evolution into a physiological wonder.

Double D: Design and Discipline

At the time this book was published, Michael Phelps was the most bemedalled athlete in Olympic history with a total of 71 medals. He won his 23rd Olympic gold medal at the 2016 Rio Olympics. It seems like nature specially designed him to be a paramount swimmer — a human marvel!

What makes Phelps unique is evident in his physique. He stands at 193 cm tall (6'4') — the ideal height for swimmers. His wingspan is a marvellous 203 cm (6'7') — 10 cm more than his height. That width, in combination with his large hands, makes for longer and more powerful strokes. His torso is longer than his legs, which decreases water resistance when swimming. Finally, he is double-jointed, and his ankles hyperextend, giving him incredible dolphin kicks that work like flippers for more powerful propulsion.

And then there's his physical response to lactate. Lactic acid present in the blood is known as *lactate*. There, it causes weakness and fatigue and directly affects recovery time. Stressful physical activities like swimming produce lactate. During Phelps' prime in the 2012 London Olympics, tests revealed that he produced less lactate, compared to his competitors and athletes in other sports. That is why he could recover so quickly. However, in an interview after the 2016 Rio Olympics, he said that with age, his recovery time had slowed down. Mitochondria, which produce cellular energy and remove lactate during exercises, decrease as we get older. He won't be able to dominate the sport forever.

Part of Phelps' competitive advantage has to do with his strength in underwater swimming, which allows for less surface resistance. Swimmers in his age group had considerably less to no training in this technique, meaning he could swim a lot faster than his peers. But, younger swimmers and their coaches caught onto his technique. Already, we see that 16- to 20-year-olds in the 2016 Rio Olympics had been trained to swim underwater from a young age.

As much as Phelps' physique and physiology helped, they were not the only reasons for his success. He also had the right mindset and discipline in training.

If those Dunedin researchers I mentioned earlier were to study his genes, I wouldn't be surprised if they found out that he too possesses the 'gene for success'.

At the peak of his training, Phelps swam 80,000 meters a week; trained five to six hours per day, six days a week; and loaded up to 12,000 calories per day to maintain his weight. His discipline, training and diet served his physique and physiology, making him an athletic wonder.

Sometimes, I wonder whether it was just his genes, or if training had a hand in shaping his body. I believe both did.

As we grow through life, we change — physically, mentally and emotionally. Changes occur naturally as a function of ageing, in response to the effects of our environment, and in the accumulation of experiences. So, I wouldn't readily agree that Phelps' body was born designed for competitive swimming.

Phelps started swimming at age seven. By the time he was 10 years old, he held a national record for his age group. At that time, he began his rigorous training. I believe that training with one of the world's leading coaches as a prepubescent child most certainly had a significant impact on his physical development.

The Sherpas and Michaels Phelps show that particular conditions can alter our physiology down to the cellular level so we can adapt. This adaptation can occur with an entire group of people over generations through constant exposure to specific elements, or more exceptionally in an individual with intense training. *Such as the case, I believe that similar conditioning can modify our body and brain for intuition and maybe even fantastical intuition?*

Does it seem like this premise is a stretch? Let me present you with another point. Have you heard of synaesthesia? Let me tell you my story.

The Colour of Music

When I was still attending university, just like any curious young adult, I went through a phase of exploring and experiencing anything I was brave enough to try. Including smoking weed.

On one occasion, the weed was so potent that I started to *see* music, even with my eyes closed. I *heard* the music, but I also *saw* it in colours. There were tunes in blue and green, but mostly in red! It was so fascinating.

I didn't know until later in my adult life that I had experienced an episode of drug-induced synaesthesia!

Synaesthesia is a crossing of sensory perceptions by which *one stimulated sense* causes unusual experiences in a *second unstimulated sense*. There are three ways to experience synaesthesia:

(1) genuine synaesthesia, which is lifelong;

(2) acquired synaesthesia, which happens after brain damage; and

(3) drug-induced synaesthesia, which is temporary during acute effects of a hallucinogen.

My experience was an example of *auditory-visual synaesthesia*, in which acoustic stimulation leads to a visual experience. It is also known as *chromaesthesia*. Hearing the music under the influence led me to see different colours.

The physiology of my senses suddenly and temporarily expanded into a more heightened and immersive experience, where hearing and seeing worked in unison. I'm not encouraging you to take drugs! However, I cannot deny that it was an extraordinary experience proving the unlimited potential of our brain, whether under an induced state or not. Perhaps in the future, we'll have legal sense-altering drugs developed for this particular purpose.

However, we don't need to wait for this to happen. A study conducted by Drs. Daniel Bor and Nicola Rothen, along with their colleagues, demonstrated that with training, adults could acquire synaesthetic experiences — without the drugs. Look them up online or at your local library if you'd like to learn more.

Environment

The Sherpas and Michael Phelps illustrate how our environment significantly impacts our genetic inheritance and contributes to skill development, including exceptional talents.

If we can inherit traits such as:

— acute senses,

— a brilliant and disciplined mind,

— a genetic predisposition to success,

— and cellular functions that give us exceptional abilities,

then it is also possible to inherit genes responsible for physiological responses such as:

— heightened perception and cognition,

— a robust neural network of quick brain power to generate instant insight,

— and a remarkable memory of cumulative data or information (also epigenetically) passed down through generations, supporting the ability to 'know without knowing how we know'.

When a conducive environment supports all these genetic inheritance, then we have the critical elements to advance powerful intuition.

I'd like to discuss the two types of environment that directly impact our development and well-being which are:

(1) the personal environment, and

(2) the social environment.

Personal Environment

I searched far and wide for the meaning of 'personal environment' based on scholarly articles and other research materials, but most of the definitions I found involved the workplace. It's not quite what I wanted to express.

I consider our *personal environment* — or personal space — that place where we can appreciate and fully express ourselves through our thoughts, feelings, values, and dreams — all those elements from within that affect our behaviour towards ourselves and others. Part of this is the proverbial *me time*, the time we spend exclusively for ourselves, to recharge, relax, and pursue our passions. We take this personal space with us wherever we go. It can quickly and significantly be influenced by our social environment. Our home is an example of a personal *and* social environment, unless we are living on our own.

Parents of young children often lose their personal environment due to the energy-intensive everyday responsibilities that demand their time and attention for many years. Some people are more inclined to experience this loss of personal environment than others, especially introverts and those living with extended family or in a demanding or unsafe community. Those working in high-pressure jobs or with difficult colleagues experience even more difficulty with finding time, space and energy for themselves.

We should not underestimate the benefits of *me time*.

It is ideal to create a sanctuary that is off-limits to others. It is a game changer that everyone should incorporate into their lives. We are not just parents, siblings, lovers, spouses, relatives, housemate, children, employees, friends, or whatever other social roles we play.

We are — first and foremost — our selves.

We are accountable for creating a harmonious and nurturing personal environment.

Part of our personal environment is our headspace. Within this quiet space lies the freedom to *hold* — or process — our thoughts and feelings. Particularly the ones we dare not share or vocalise, those we wouldn't want another soul to know. It is the depository of our secrets, insecurities, fears, biases and prejudices, grudges, bitterness, and whatever else may be lurking. Herein our desires, wishes, prayers, hopes, and beliefs also take root, and the individual connections we have to our world, invisible and intangible as they may be.

Social Environment

University of Wisconsin Professor and Author Karen K Kirst-Ashman defines the social environment as 'the sum total of social and cultural conditions, circumstances, and human interactions that encompass human beings'.

We find ourselves in a social environment wherever people are. It starts with the general family environment where we grew up, especially during the critical formative years, and goes on to cover our education, work, culture, economics, and communities — from local to global, including the processes and technologies that govern them. It is dynamic and always changing as a result of personal and environmental factors,

Our social environment defines the external world to which we belong, where we contribute our time, energy, and other resources, and how we are affected as members of society. It impacts our lives and influences our perception significantly enough to mould us as individuals, by forming our behaviours and cognitive functions, including intuition.

According to the Scottish Public Health Observatory, our behaviour, relationships, gender and ethnic group, the conditions and communities in which we live, and how we feel about ourselves are all elements of the social environment.

If we live in poverty, we focus on survival. We have only one thing in mind — to find food and shelter, and all of our energy will be expended towards making it through to the next day or the next meal. Anything else might seem like unnecessary noise or an alien concept.

If we live with sceptics or negativity, then we find it difficult to trust people. Perhaps even ourselves. It is easy to become jaded, pessimistic, frustrated, angry or bitter. We may become aggressive as a defence mechanism, or timid and self-doubting, as a consequence of a damaging social environment.

Naturally, if we would like to nurture ourselves and our intuition, it is important to recognise our social environments and ensure that we are surrounded by supportive people who share or appreciate our interests. We make that happen by choosing and managing the physical environment in which we live and being mindful of the company we keep — including family members, friends and colleagues.

Our social environment can make or break us by keeping in check or switching on our genetic and epigenetic predispositions as we progress in life, such as the case of James Fallon.

The Heart and the Hearth

James Fallon is a well-known neuroscientist who has been studying the brains of psychopaths for more than 27 years. He discovered that psychopaths have low activity in regions of the brain's frontal and temporal lobes linked to empathy, morality and self-control. Fallon also discovered that psychopaths have a gene called the MAOA gene associated with aggression and violence. He also made the startling discovery that he has both — the psychopathic brain and the MAOA gene. Fallon was born a psychopath. However, he is nonviolent, stable, accomplished, and a well-respected professional.

Fallon used to believe that our genetic makeup foretells our future or destiny. But based on his own life and predisposition to violence, Fallon now understands that *the combination of nature and nurture, and our free will are what define us.*

In Fallon's NPR interview with Glynn Washington, he said that he thinks his wonderful childhood may have made all the difference. His parents doted on him, and he had a loving relationship with his siblings and extended family. Because of that, he is always mindful of how he interacts with people, especially with his family. *It's this consistent reinforcement of mindfulness that keeps his natural tendency dormant and in check.*

Culture

Culture is part of our environment. *Oxford Living Dictionary* calls it 'the ideas, customs, and social behaviour of a particular people or society'. The University of Minnesota further defines culture in two manners. *Nonmaterial culture* 'includes the values, beliefs, symbols and, language that define a society'. And then there is the *material culture* made up of 'all the society's physical objects, such as its tools and technology, clothing, eating utensils, and means of transportation'.

How we perceive ourselves as individuals and as members of society, and how we see the world, are significantly influenced by culture. The East and West view the individual and the world through different eyes, affecting perception and reasoning, which profoundly impacts the path to developing intuition.

Jeong-Ook Lee, Myung-jin Kim and their colleagues conducted a study in the US, the UK, and East Asia that showed culture's influence on our thought processes, as well as the context of our interaction with others, from our sense of self and society, to how we behave in social and business settings.

They noted that Westerners see the world as a collection of separate individual objects, which is why they tend to classify and categorise things based on similar properties, going all the way back to Plato and Aristotle. They see the world as individually expressed nouns.

Easterners see the world as a big field where everything is related and interconnected. Life is expressed as verbs that represent the interactions between objects.

The Gist of the Matter

I was born and raised in the Philippines. Thus, I came from a *high-context culture* which is mostly influenced by relationships with others. For as long as I can remember, I've always been straightforward and particular about expressing myself concerning my values, which would fit better in a *low-context culture*. The way I communicated and interacted with others proved challenging while I was growing up. Instead of being seen as honest and truthful, I was apparently a tactless youngster.

In such a culture, it is always important to consider how others would feel about the words that you use, so I had to learn to be diplomatic and tactful, regardless of how long-winded the conversations might become. If I wanted continuous cooperation and a harmonious relationship, maintaining tact was necessary. Otherwise, I could hurt someone's honour and pride.

Education is a big deal in Filipino culture — which school you attend, what you study, and when you finish. Completing a degree brings honour, prestige, and hope for the family, the possibility of a better life. It's not unusual for parents to toil day and night or to borrow money from usurers (people who charge money at sky-high interest rates) in order to pay for school fees and ensure their kids finish university. Once the older kids graduate, they are expected to do their share and send the younger siblings to school until they, in turn, get their degrees, and so on.

We show respect to anyone who is older. Being older presumably means more life experience and wisdom, thus a higher position in the family or community. I remember our practice of *pagmamano* (kissing the hands of our elders) come 6pm, which is the time for the *Angelus*, a Catholic prayer. I am pretty sure the practice ceased a long time ago. At any rate, it is not happening in my home.

However, respect for others is still very important in the Philippines and can be seen when addressing others. We use Sir or Ma'am, Tita (Auntie) or Tito (Uncle), Lola (Grandma) and Lolo (Grandpa), and Ate (elder sister) or Kuya (older brother). We also use the words *po*, *opo*, and *ho* as a sign of respect.

Our cultural context is all about relationships. It's no surprise that we have great extended families, more like clans in reality. It seems like everyone from the same province is related. We acknowledge even our fourth cousins, and we usually hear introductions go something like, 'This is so-and-so, the daughter of your mom's third cousin from her father side.'

Of course, for the most part, these customs are great because they acknowledge many generations of the family tree and encourage closeness and belonging. It also presents us with that select group of people we can count on when help is needed.

However, nothing is perfect, and there will always be downsides to these gracious customs. One example is when a relative from the province comes to visit the city and needs a place to stay. All is well if everyone behaves considerately of each other. The challenge lies when they outstay their welcome, which sometimes happens. But who can blame them? It is always a big thing, in a positive way, when family visits. We make sure we cook the best food, bring out the best dinnerware, give them the best bed in the house, and help them in every which way we can. These gestures are made out of the kindness of one's heart and with much respect.

However, this is naturally unsustainable in the long term. Plenty of advance notice helps us prepare, but there is a time and a place that a visit runs its course. In situations like this, we can only hope that the relative would be considerate enough to know when it is time to leave. Otherwise, regardless of how much we have done, hurt feelings and pride are the very likely results.

It is customary to invite anyone we know, out of courtesy and generosity, to eat with us if they chance upon us while eating/dining at home, at work or in restaurants. It is the same essence behind opening one's house to everyone, including strangers, to dine together and share the blessings during 'fiestas' in the provinces. These *fiestas* are very important and celebrated as a form of thanksgiving to the town's or city's patron saint. And of course, food is abundant and available to everyone.

By the same token and as a consequence, occasionally rivalries arise between neighbours concerning who has the best *handa* (prepared food, drinks, booze, etc.). Some people even go into debt trying to keep up with the Juans and Marias during fiestas. At least, that was how it was when I was growing up. I'm not sure how it is now, considering I've lived almost half of my adult life overseas.

I love the Filipino culture — its warmth, hospitality, respect for others, kindness, generosity, and gratitude. I also embrace the lessons I learned from its downside. I learned to be practical and sensible, NOT to spend beyond my means, to set boundaries, and *to appreciate myself because I AM also important*.

I believe that coming from a high-context culture helped me become more intuitive with my understanding of how other people feel and think. I see this through their facial expressions, body language, intonations and the words they use.

As I have matured and lived and travelled abroad, I have had the opportunity to see and experience many other cultures. I've learned how food can be a bridge, a source of joy and goodwill, and a shared passion, not just in the Philippines but across the oceans.

Having a basic understanding of cultural differences has helped me manoeuvre my way around. I've learned to read between the lines or fill in the blanks in my interactions with others.

Some would argue that I have become assuming. On the contrary, by paying attention to the context of communication, I have learned to intuit or 'sense' others.

I have come to appreciate that wherever I go, there exists a universal culture which embraces listening, empathy, warmth, genuineness, compassion, and altruism. I believe that cultural knowledge and appreciation of a place and its people are invaluable to intuiting.

Voices

Culture sets the environment for intuition to grow. The mind is the space where culture impacts intuition the most.

In a collectivist and high-context culture, the mind expands beyond what is seen and spoken. Understanding transcends the tangible and the living. In many eastern cultures, the ancestors who have passed on are venerated and believed to influence the living during significant life events. Some feel their ancestors' handiwork on a daily basis.

This belief in that which is unseen is liberating and creates a meaningful connection that affects a person's thought process, making it less rigid, more imaginative, and open to developing intuition.

It is hospitable in such a way that the practice of consulting, asking for guidance and advice, engaging in a conversation with the dearly departed, and hearing them back, is not something to fear or worry.

Schizophrenia is not only genetically inherited, but it is also profoundly influenced by culture. The cultural connection is evident in a study on schizophrenia and its different manifestations between the East and West.

A study conducted by Stanford University Anthropology Professor Dr TM Luhrmann and her colleagues revealed that 'hearing voices' is immediately regarded as a symptom of this mental disorder in the US, which is a low-context and individualist culture. Diagnosed patients describe the voices they hear as nasty, disgusting, violent and harmful. Therefore, these patients do not engage with them. In fact, they get medications to suppress them.

Interviews revealed that patients in the East have no problem engaging with their voices. In fact, they say that the voices often give them helpful and beneficial tasks like 'go take a shower and clean'. The majority of these patients know the voices as their kin, providing advice and even keeping them company when lonely. Some associate these voices as the voice of God or the angels. What they experience is not perceived immediately as psychosis, but potentially a form of spiritual experience.

The Philippines is a predominantly Christian country. People believe in God, the divine and the supernatural. They think that their dearly departed ancestors and loved ones act as a bridge. They are the intercessors between the living and their God, and available for the prayers and supplications of their descendants, especially in dire times of need.

Answered prayers or positive outcomes — such as being pulled out of harm's way or overcoming a challenging situation — could be intuition at work.

Or intuition could be how God communicates.

Experiences and Development

Memorable. Awful. Fantastic. We tend to simplify our experiences by applying a limited vocabulary of adjectives. Perhaps it is because most of our experiences are pretty much the same every day. We don't generally notice or describe what has become mundane, so we are not accustomed to talking about what happens around us.

When we are working on paying attention and being *mindful,* we might try to focus on the minutest detail of the experience we are having, such as our breathing, rather than the entirety of the experience itself.

We take for granted the fact that the accumulation and frequency of our experiences give us a degree of proficiency in whatever we experience. We are meant to appreciate and learn from life always, be it:

— the monotonous rhythm of everyday life;

— those splendid once-in-a-lifetime experiences; or even

— the painful transformations that bring forth endings and beginnings.

When we pay attention to life, we gain not only proficiency but also maturity.

I believe maturity is immanent in wisdom, as wisdom is immanent in intuition.

Where we are in life's stages impacts how we see ourselves and the world, and how open and receptive we are to intuition.

CHILDHOOD (0–12 YEARS)

From childhood to prepubescence, we are dependent on our caregivers. How we are taken care of leaves a lasting effect on our lives. What we experience at this stage is very much all about 'ME'.

When all goes well, our experiences help us form a good basic understanding of ourselves as individuals, and hopefully as part of society — made up of family, friends and school. At this stage, we begin to appreciate loyalty, good company, and reliability in our childhood friends. Friendships nurtured can grow into lifelong bonds. Our experiences could present challenges to our development and understanding of who we are if we are placed in a confusing, chaotic, or less-than-nurturing-and-loving environment.

PUBERTY TO YOUNG ADULTHOOD (13–29 YEARS)

From puberty to young adulthood, our bodies experience amazing and profound changes due to chemical processes. We experience remarkable growth spurts, and an intensity of our emotions, thoughts and actions — most notably regarding the discovery of how romantic relationships work. We finish school, leave home, start a career, and become our own person. The focus of 'ME' now evolves to 'ME + whoever is in my life where I am'.

We develop from crushes to puppy love to serious romantic relationships. We can compare ourselves to pioneering explorers of this life stage, where we discover the firsts of many things. These discoveries are always attached to lessons. However, due to our lack of maturity, we are unable to retain and uphold experiences as lessons learned, regardless of how intensely we feel. As such, we can find ourselves continually setting patterns in life that will remain until we learn from them.

ADULTHOOD (30–49 YEARS)

As we further our journey to adulthood, we become full-fledged adults hoping not to become our parents. That phrase, 'hoping not to become our parents', shouldn't be viewed negatively. It is practical and progressive. We examine what we want to achieve, how we express ourselves, and learn to become more 'us' than 'our parents' offspring'. This stage often leads to self-sufficiency. We immerse ourselves in creating a life of our own. Many of our experiences centre on transition and putting down roots. We may:

— travel,

— settle down,

— get into a loving and stable partnership,

— create our own family,

— raise kids,

— balance work and personal life along with our relationships and responsibilities.

Some of us have painful experiences, like losing a loved one or coming to the end of a romantic relationship. These challenging times usually usher in a *transformation* or *awakening* translating to a significant leap in wisdom and maturity.

At this stage, our experiences lead us to assess or reassess our life's purpose. We hope that we not only recognise and release the unresolved patterns that we set in early adult life, but appreciate and hold onto the lessons attached to them. Doing this allows us to create, pay attention to and be sensitive to new patterns.

If by the middle to end of this stage, we still have not begun to sort out old unwanted patterns, it becomes more challenging. Our failure to resolve that which we must let go of means that we are profoundly stuck — and achieving mastery in staying stuck. I don't know about you, but mastery in staying stuck is not a skill I want to possess. For how are we able to appreciate or have the chance to experience anything new when we have lost ourselves in a pile of old experiences that keep us from going anywhere?

This stage in life is abundant with opportunities to become wise. It is multifaceted, focused on 'ME + FAMILY + the outside world'. We should seize them.

MIDDLE AGE THROUGH ONSET OF RETIREMENT (50–69)

In later adulthood, we make the most of things. We are not quite at the end of our journey but know that all too soon we will be. We value our health, our families, and a level of skill and expertise in our careers, and we realise that we had better make the most of our time. We continue to experience growth and spend a lot of time on self-reflection. We anticipate and prepare for retirement. If in our thirties and forties we found ourselves more immersed in the lives of others (children, spouse, colleagues, etc.) than invested in ourselves, this stage in life finds us refocused on ourselves. Our experiences are now mostly aligned with productivity, purpose, meaning, legacy and self-worth.

By the time we reach our fifties, our thoughts and emotions stabilise. We prefer things that are steadfast and reliable. There is still an intensity motivated by the passions in our life — hobbies, projects, the people who are closest to our heart — but with a maturity that makes us appreciate them better. The passions we have now are those that linger and inspire.

At this point, our experiences have made us confident in listening to our intuition. *We know that something is right because it feels right.* Hopefully, by now we know what *feels right* means to us.

We experience our kids leaving home and spreading their wings. We become grandparents. We begin to retire and finally finding plenty of time for ourselves. All of which can bring a different kind of anxiety or nervousness because part of it means we are nearing the last stage of life's journey.

For some, this is a time to experience a renaissance and a realignment of purpose with the gift of time in our hands.

Death becomes familiar as we lose a number of friends, colleagues and loved ones around the same age group, and those who are older. We start to ease into the idea of our own mortality and transience, which creates many questions about life that only self-reflection can answer. How well are we living life?

Experiencing the loss of a loved one can be both cathartic and catalytic. It triggers a personal 'awakening' and opens us up to a full breadth of intense emotions and thoughts that swing from one end of the spectrum to the other. This awakening is responsible for a change in perspective, often manifested in a better and deeper appreciation of our circumstances, the people we love and of ourselves. This shift is wisdom gained. This process breathes strength to our intuition.

GOLDEN YEARS (65–EARLY 70s)

In our golden years, which set in after retirement around 65 to 70, we may experience a renewed sense of adventure. We have the time to finally do and enjoy the things we have desired, yet put aside because of our responsibilities. We start to shift from prioritising responsibilities to others to prioritising responsibilities to ourselves. Particularly if in good health, we should find a renewed lust for life.

OLDER ADULTHOOD (70 AND UP)

From our seventies onward, we exhibit courage every day because we know that our time is limited. At this point, we have become pillars of our family, offering words of wisdom to children and grandchildren, nieces and nephews., We give back to society, pursue our passions, rediscover ourselves, and appreciate the life we are living. Our bodies might be getting old; our cognition might start to diminish, yet we still find happiness and positivity as we move forward.

I believe that for as long as we are *compos mentis* (of sound mind), this stage is also the golden age of intuition. We have experienced, learned and retained much knowledge, which translates to a deeper mastery of life. We have strong intuition — the ability to 'know without knowing how we know'. It is like becoming a chess grandmaster who can anticipate many moves ahead. It becomes harder to explain how we know our next move, yet we are quite confident that our decision is right, whatever the outcome.

I remember a Filipino saying I grew up with, passed down from my elders, which described that wisdom and mastery that comes from age and experience: *Papunta ka pa lang, naka-ilang balik na ako.* It means, 'You're just starting your journey, but I have been there and back many times over.'

Intuition is the offspring of our experiences focusing on the evolution of our relationships — whether with ourselves, others or the world itself.

It grows from an honest appreciation of what truly matters and the people we love, creating a reliable compass that helps us navigate life. Especially the grey areas.

Memory, Learning and Identity

Let's recap, shall we? So far, we've covered the first three quadrants of ZIQ2 — inheritance, environment and experience.

Genes remember and execute the instructions to create us into breathing, functioning human beings. Epigenetics recognises the conditions of our environment that affect the instructions in our genes significantly. Our physiology is the manifestation of these instructions translated into physical systems, processes and functions that enable us to perform tasks on a daily basis. Culture, age, our environment and our experience shape how we perceive and react to the world and to each other, and shape what and how we intuit.

Now, I want to talk about the fourth and final quadrant: memory.

Memories, whether inherited or experienced, form our unique identities. They are critical to acquired wisdom. They store the highlights of and patterns in our lives, which we can either keep and enhance to improve our circumstances, or recognise and use to resolve issues and move forward. Our memories make our intuition bank stronger and more mature.

Memory is a huge part of our self-identity and our ability to respond to the world around us and access intuition. When we experience gaps in memory, life becomes more difficult, and we may not be at a level or capacity to be intuitive.

There are people with amnesia who have had a large part of their memory wiped out, affecting their sense of identity and making them feel lost.

Then there are those whose overall memory is intact but suffer from gaps — particularly childhood memories. This is the case for many adopted children. They may feel lost and incomplete. Once they reach adulthood, many adopted children have a desire to find their biological parents and fill the gaps surrounding their birth and family history.

Others suffer from mental illness such as Alzheimer's or dementia. They have forgotten themselves and the people around them. We hear how difficult it is for both the patient and their family members, who bear witness to the ever-widening gap in their loved one's life between who and what they were and who and what they've become. Memories, expertise and identity disappear. The manifestations of this disease are intuition's nightmare.

Every time we are called upon to use a skill, we retrieve it from our memory bank and practice conscious competence. With constant use, we push it towards unconscious competence — a response that is automatic and second nature.

Memory can be mystical.

Sometimes scientists cannot explain the root of memories. We find many such cases on YouTube and across the internet. The most remarkable cases involve children accessing the memory of their past lives, including the way they died. In one particular case reported by Tara MacIsaac for *The Epoch Times*, a three-year-old boy recalled being murdered in his previous life. He led police to both the skeleton and the murder weapon — an axe.

Memory can be fantastical.

There are extraordinary cases of people with absolutely no proficiency in a particular skill who become instantly specialised after suffering head trauma, gaining language, music, science or mathematical skills.

Rueben Nsemoh, an American teenager who suffered a head injury playing soccer and fell into a three-day coma, woke up speaking fluent Spanish but struggling to speak his native English. There are stories in newspapers about an Englishman speaking Welsh after a stroke, a Croatian girl speaking German after a coma, an Australian speaking Mandarin after a car crash, and an Italian speaking French after a brain injury. In each case, the second language had been studied briefly at some point in the subjects' lives, but they were far from fluent.

Then there is Jason Padgett who suffered a severe concussion and post-traumatic stress disorder (PTSD) and ended up with *savant syndrome,* a rare medical condition sometimes described as 'island of genius'. The man who had never progressed beyond pre-algebra could now see shapes and angles everywhere. Today he is an artist who draws fractals and representations of pi.

Finally, there is Derek Amato, another *savant syndrome* patient. He suffered severe head trauma after a pool diving incident. Before the injury, he dabbled in guitar and said he played at about a 2.5 on a scale of 1–10. He now plays the piano like a virtuoso and sees patterns stream across his brain. It all started when he went to a friends house and felt drawn to the piano. He sat down and could play.

Those who remember past lives are mostly very young and less experienced in life. Their minds are fresh and innocent, and nothing seems impossible. They make me think of the headspace I require for my Tarot readings, akin to a 'blank canvas'.

The savants who suffered head trauma experienced a change in brain structure, which made them hyper specialised. The cause is known. But the exact reason or way in which they are able to access such high levels proficiency in previously unaccessible skills eludes scientists.

Cases of mystical and fantastical memory lead me back to the idea of 'collective consciousness or unconsciousness'. I imagine these children and patients must have greater access to the same repository of collective experience that is supposedly available to everyone. But the altered state and structure of their brains somehow deepens access and permits them to retrieve memories of past lives or gain hyper specialised competencies.

I once read an article in *Scientific American* about the *morphic field,* or 'extended mind', as hypothesised by Rupert Sheldrake, a prominent biologist. In the interview, he said that 'all self-organising systems, such as molecules, crystals, cells, plants, animals and animal societies, have a collective memory on which each draws and to which it contributes'.

Scientific proof of such a remarkable repository of collective memories is highly remote at this time, but maybe future generations will find a method to prove it. For now, I have to remember what the brilliant mathematician, logician and philosopher Kurt Gödel's

Incompleteness Theorems mean to me, that even the most rigorous logic of math — and science for that matter — have their limitations, and hence cannot be used to prove everything. There is always more to discover, more to learn. Our view of life remains incomplete, and proof is predicated on that which we cannot see.

In the meantime, we have some workable scientific evidence now, so let's go back to the basic understanding of memory. According to *The Human Memory* website, 'Memory is our ability to encode, store, retain and subsequently recall information and past experiences in the human brain. It can be thought of in general terms as the use of past experience to affect or influence current behaviour.'

Many of us prefer to hold on to happy memories only. They give us a sense of great joy and uplift us. But when traumatic memories are deeply buried as a coping mechanism to protect our psyche and well-being, they can actually impede our health and well-being. Bringing them to the surface, with the help of a health professional, can be liberating and give us a sense of closure towards complete healing.

It's tricky to share the memory of an event with a friend or family member because we may remember things so differently. Remember our discussion about perception? Memories carry power because of our perceptual uniqueness. We assign layers of truth to any memory, based on our perception, emotions, and other experiences that combine in impact.

Sometimes, we can create false memories to escape blame, deny the truth, alleviate our guilt, idealise or romanticise a loved one who has passed away, protect ourselves from fear and anxiety, or for a variety of other reasons.

Memory, regardless of how magical and fantastical it can be at its most amazing, can also be inaccurate and unreliable. Hence, it's futile to obsess over details. Here are some pointers to overcome this tendency. It serves us best to:

(1) rise above the specifics, and instead

(2) hone in on the lessons and the wisdom that pave the way towards adaptation, competence and mastery.

(3) By engaging our memory with our imagination in a constructive and creative manner, we are able to

(4) test and push the boundaries of what is possible.

When done regularly, pointers 1 to 4 are akin to creating an inner mentor who is omnipresent, illuminating the various paths to finer intuition.

Part 3: The Practicalities of Intuition

Chapter 4   The Dependencies of Intuition

When we mention the phrase 'developing our intuition', it is normal to jump to the idea of training, practice and dedication, much in the same way that we would develop athletic or academic abilities. We've all heard the phrase 'practice makes perfect'.

But while it is true that these training, practice and dedication help intuition develop, we need to know where to focus, how to get started, and the necessary resources to engage. Otherwise, it would be like sending someone out to play rugby without first teaching them what to do with the ball, how to score, the dimensions of the field, or any of the rules of the game. They wouldn't know where to start.

The number one resource we often ignore, overlook or deem inconsequential is the most critical — ourself!

Unfortunately, the same attitude and line of thinking that causes us to discount ourselves as teacher and guide is a primary reason that we are often unsuccessful at raising our intuition to the next level.

Everything about us:

— who and how we are as a person

— how we practice self-care

— how we think,

represents the dependencies of intuition.

So we better start with getting to know ourselves better.

Know Thyself

I married and had children young. I had to stop pursuing my degree in order to take care of my kids and earn a living. I remember how difficult it was. I felt like I'd had to fast forward from childhood to adulthood, and I know I missed out on many experiences that would have helped me develop and create a better understanding of myself.

I come from a low-income family, so I made sure that when I had kids, they would have more than what I had growing up. I soldiered on despite feeling down and tired very often.

'Impossible' was a word that did not exist in my vocabulary. I took things as they came, regardless of the difficulties, and strived hard every day to provide for my children. But there was a fundamental problem: I forgot about myself.

I had so lost myself in the process of raising a family that I missed all the signs that I was falling into depression. I was already in its teeth when I realised what had happened. By losing myself, I had silenced the intuition that would have warned me.

I was no good to anyone. I couldn't be there for myself. Consequently, I couldn't be there for my children. They are adults now, and sometimes we remember together. Talking about it is hard and heavy. Without getting drawn to the memory and diminishing the experience, we try to find humour in my disagreeable behaviour back then.

Losing or forgetting one's self is similar to an internally combustible bomb that is precarious, all-consuming and very disruptive. When we lose our sense of self, nothing else matters. The people we love the most become invisible to us, for how can we see them when we cannot even see ourselves?

I remember Nanay before and after she broke up with her long-time boyfriend. She used to take care of herself. She would dress smartly, put on some light makeup and make sure she looked good. A free spirit, she was usually out with her many friends. She was rarely at home when I was a teenager.

After the breakup, she stopped caring. Days would pass between showers. She stayed at home and quit socialising with her friends. She would forget to eat and just stare into space for hours on end.

I was the same during my depression, or maybe worse because I had no friends. And I was ashamed to reach out to my Lola Mommy and other family members.

In hindsight, had I known then what I know now, I could have taken care of myself better, or at least sought help sooner. Had I recognised my mom's predisposition, I would have realised it was also mine. It was a critical aspect that I needed to understand about myself.

How well do you know yourself?

You could answer 'I don't know myself very well at all', 'a little', 'not sure', 'well', or 'very well'. Or maybe even — 'what do you mean?'.

If we reflect on the question, we may realise the enormity and profundity of the scope of what constitutes one's self. It's easy to feel anxious when confronted by it because we may not fully know the answer. And not knowing leaves a huge, gaping hole which needs to filled. We need to identify what's missing in our self-knowledge and work to fill in the blanks before we can honestly assess who we are.

Now that we are talking about *knowing thyself* in the context of developing intuition, we can look to ZIQ1 and ZIQ2 for answers.

In previous chapters, I presented how our family lines dramatically affect many aspects of our individuality.

Now is the time to get to know the personalities in your family tree and make an effort to understand that part of yourself. Get into the practice of being inquisitive about Grandma, Grandpa, Mom and Dad, even aunts and uncles. I know that as you get into this exercise, you will see family patterns and predispositions emerge that you could already be experiencing in your life.

It is important to know their circumstances and how they took care of themselves in terms of diet, lifestyle, culture, upbringing, beliefs, strengths, weaknesses, illnesses, tendencies, challenges they faced, and the environment in which they lived. All of these elements will contribute to a clearer picture of what ZIQ2 looks like for you.

As you get to know your ancestors, you will get to know yourself better. Hopefully, you can use this knowledge to be more mindful of your own experiences and the thought processes in your daily life.

Health and Lifestyle

We need to maintain a healthy mind and body to add new experiences to the intuition bank.

For how can we perceive accurately if:

> — our senses are weak;

> — we are distracted by palpitations or an irregular heartbeat from, say, drinking too much caffeine or from a heart ailment;

— we have a vague memory or lousy recollection due to a lack of sleep, excessive alcohol consumption, excessive drug use, or some health issues; and

— our thought processes are dark, gloomy, and cynical?

These are just some of the many examples that interfere with and even block intuition. It is logical to sort out our health concerns and be dedicated to maintaining a reasonable level of overall physical and mental fitness before we commit to train and practice intuition.

Diet and Essential Nutrients

After months of blissful ignorance, I weighed myself recently and was shocked to find that I had reached a personal record-breaking weight of 61 kg. For my frame and height, that is a lot of excess weight! I could easily blame my perimenopausal stage for out-of-whack hormones and an insatiable hunger for sweets like cakes, chocolate and ice cream. But truly, I can only blame myself. Weight gain is the logical consequence of my overindulgence.

If it's any consolation (to myself), the weight-shock woke me up! I started to pay more attention to what I eat. I'm in the process of experimenting and finding the best combination of food groups that works for me. At the moment, I still eat fatty and sweet stuff, but the healthy ones. I do my best to have nuts, cacao, fish, fruits and salad. I have to do this. Otherwise, I will limit my health and quality of life, and be vulnerable to diseases that run in my family, like heart ailments and cancer. How can I nurture intuition if I'm sick?

When we are at of childbearing age, our diet affects us as well as our offspring — children and grandchildren — through epigenetics. I sometimes wonder how my kids will be affected by what I ate when I was pregnant with them. I certainly remember I avoided sugary foods and smoking, and I strictly followed the advice of my wonderful ob-gyn. But what about what I ate before and after pregnancy? OMG!

Don't worry. Scientists say a healthy diet can reverse epigenetic changes in our genes, and beneficially affect our physiology and predispositions to diseases. Whew, that's comforting to know!

We need to look at eating in a different light, especially when we want to create and raise a family. It is sobering to realise that we are not just eating for ourselves, but also for our future generations.

By eating for health, we can reduce the stress, fatigue, aches and pains that come with not taking care of ourselves and focus on the better things in life. We can be receptive to the processes associated with intuition.

Since our body, particularly our senses and brain are part of these processes, let's look at nutrients we can add to our diet, particularly those that keep our body and senses healthy and our memory sharp.

A full list of healthy foods that contain the nutrients listed on the following pages can be found at the end of this section, on page 122.

Brain

When I was a kid, people always thought I was way mature for my age, based on the manner I thought and spoke. Well, that may be. I've thought a lot about it, and I think I know why. It may be that my diet played a major role in that impression.

Growing up in a family with limited financial resources meant we could only eat meat occasionally because it was expensive. I resented my folks for often giving me fish and green vegetables. Though money was just enough for the necessities, my Lola Mommy made sure I always had cod liver oil supplement, in emulsion form, which was rich in Omega-3 fatty acids. I used to gag drinking it. As soon as I had it in my mouth, my throat would function like it had a mind of its own - constricting to stop the liquid from going down. It seemed my body preferred to suffocate and die rather than swallow that devilry! A spoonful was enough to make my eyes water from the overpowering fishy taste, and the smell that escaped and reeked out of my nose. Kids nowadays are lucky to have their supplements taste like lollies. But Lola Mommy knew best. I'm sure the fish and vegetable diet — and the cod liver oil supplement — helped my developing brain tremendously. The torment was well worth it.

According to experts, Omega-3 fatty acids are proven to be effective in reducing depression, schizophrenia and bipolar disorders, when combined with exercise. People suffering from these mental illnesses may be deficient in this nutrient, which definitely could have been the case with Nanay and me when we were ill.

How does Omega-3 work?

Our bodies produce cortisol which, in healthy amounts, is beneficial to many bodily functions. It reduces stress, maintains steady blood sugar level, regulates metabolism and aids in memory formation, to name a few. But, during prolonged periods of mental stress, our bodies produce more of it, and that can cause problems.

According to *University Health News*, prolonged periods of high cortisol levels can lead to many health problems including depression, fatigue, lack of focus or decreased concentration, weight gain, obesity, insomnia, irritability, high blood pressure, and high blood sugar.

Omega-3 fatty acids from fish oil have been proven to reduce the excess cortisol and other chemicals produced by the body. Together with Omega-6 fatty acids, Omega-3s have been known to promote healthy ageing, brain functions and cognition. Folate — a natural form of vitamin B9 — and folic acid — the synthetic version of folate found in supplements and used to fortify food — have also shown a lot of promise in preventing cognitive decline and dementia in ageing.

We can now understand how Omega-3 and Omega-6 fatty acids, and folate and folic acid, work well to maintain a healthy brain. However, anything too much or too little of any of these nutrients is problematic. Always remember that moderation is key.

Of course, it's not just the brain that we need to take care of. We also need our sensory organs to be strong and healthy, for they are responsible for perception — the first process to intuiting. The healthier our senses are, the better we perceive.

Eyes

I love a British brand of prescription glasses known for the funny commercials that they make, all about the challenges of visual misperception. There's a particularly good one about a man who enters the steam-filled room of a hotel that he perceives to be the sauna. He walks in, removes his towel, sits down in his birthday suit, and makes himself comfortable, only slightly confused by a carrot on the bench where he is seated. As the smoke dissipates, everything becomes clear. There is no sauna. Instead, he finds himself in the kitchen of a famous British celebrity chef, who is none-too-happy upon seeing a stark naked man in his kitchen, and promptly — and menacingly — chops a sausage. It is hilarious! Go to YouTube, look up *Specsavers 'Sauna' Advert* and take a look. Enjoy!

I can relate in a way, except that I still have hawk-eyed vision because I'm farsighted. Nowadays, my husband loves to tease and mimic me when I squint to read because I refuse to be defeated by my reading glasses. Seriously, I found that the more I relied on my reading glasses, the lazier my eyes became and more blurred my vision got. (I'm not saying not to wear your glasses.)

As we reach 40, the muscles in our body, including our eyes, become less flexible, and most of us would need eyeglasses, at least for reading. While I continue to resist, my husband seems to be getting to that stage.

To keep our eyes as healthy as possible, it is good to do eye exercises, which are readily available online. It's best to make sure we eat the right nutrients to keep them healthy and see our optometrist or ophthalmologist for regular checkups.

It is vital we take care of our eyes because they are our window to the world and our brain.

On a daily basis, our eyes help us see and evaluate:
- body language when communicating with others,
- our environment for signs of threat, and
- visual associations that help us intuit.

Our eyes can also reveal our brain's health years before cognitive decline or other predispositions to other brain deficiencies become evident.

Moreover, many of us require a healthy sense of sight for use in our professions or vocations that require us to see fine details. Some examples include:

— artist,

— detective or investigator,

— builder or carpenter,

— voice actor,

— proofreader or editor,

— photographer,

— research scientist,

— mathematician.

There are certainly successful people in many of these fields who are not sighted, or who have lost their sense of sight, but it it is helpful.

Artists are pretty intuitive in expressing how they perceive the world in their artwork. It is fascinating to recognise how it may be similar to or different from our own view of the world — especially if there is a remarkable distinction.

A sense of sight is crucial to so much of what we perceive. I think of Monet and Degas. Both suffered a loss of vision, Degas from what was likely age-related macular degeneration and Monet from cataracts, which manifested in their paintings. Degas' later work lacked his usual detail. Monet painted yellow for a while until he had the lens in his left eye removed in cataract surgery, and then he started painting in blue, apparently from seeing ultraviolet waves of light, as many birds, insects and animals perceive.

Leafy green vegetables and foods rich in Omega-3 fatty acids contain many valuable nutrients beneficial to our eyes. Vitamins A, C, and E are also essential for ocular health.

Vitamin A protects the cornea and, combined with C, E, beta-carotene, copper and zinc, decreases the risk of age-related macular degeneration (AMD) and the formation of cataracts. Combined, vitamins A and C promote healthy blood vessels such as the delicate capillaries of the retina and maintain connective tissues like the collagen found in the cornea.

Omega-3 fatty acids may protect adult eyes from age-related macular degeneration (AMD), high eye pressure, glaucoma, and dry eye syndrome. AMD causes the majority of vision loss for people over 50 years old. Dry eye syndrome happens when there is lack of lubrication and moisture in the form of tears. It leads to irritation, swelling and even scarring on the surface of the eyes.

Ears

Equally important to our eyes are our ears, which allow us to receive and interpret sounds in order to communicate. They help us translate vibrational frequencies into comprehensible information. The noise from an approaching train or vehicle can represent possible danger. Music can be exhilarating or relaxing. A baby's cry or a cat's meow can signify hunger. Our ears maintain our sense of balance and allow us to connect and appreciate our world so much more — most especially through music and the sounds of nature.

Musicians are highly intuitive and interpretive individuals. I am especially awed with those who play by ear. They can quickly place notes or chords, just by listening, and have a level of unconscious competence that makes the process natural, automatic and effortless. A decline in hearing would be devastating to such a musician, I'm sure.

Hearing loss is a problem all over the world, primarily due to ageing, noise pollution and the damaging practice of listening to loud music with headsets.

I can't imagine how I would feel if I were to stop hearing the sound of ocean waves, the chirping of birds, the rustling of leaves, the voices of my loved ones, the meow of my fur baby, and the many other sounds that connect me to the rest of the world.

A couple of years ago, I finished my Postgraduate Diploma in Business, and I was supposed to fly to Invercargill, New Zealand for my graduation. However, a couple of days before, I woke up with my world spinning. I was extremely dizzy and found it hard to keep my balance. I had to cancel my flight and go to a doctor.

I was diagnosed with vertigo, most probably linked to a disturbance in my inner ear. It took a couple of months and some exercises to get back to normal. I remember it was worse when getting in and out of bed, so I had to do that slowly. I learned from a cousin that this runs on the father side of my family. My paternal grandmother, who had vertigo later in life, lost her hearing and developed dementia. Recently, scientists have said that treating hearing loss may prevent the onset of cognitive decline and dementia. Some of my aunts and one cousin have vertigo too. This makes me also predisposed to it. Not to mention adding this to my other predispositions. Whew!

By golly, what should we do then? Of course, avoiding harmful noises is a common sense preventative measure and top priority. We also need to include in our diet many of the same vital nutrients that keep our eyes healthy, such as a daily intake of beta-carotene, vitamins C and E, and magnesium, all of which are proven to be beneficial to our ears.

Be advised that some food and drinks may make things worse, depending on your predispositions to certain ear illnesses. For instance, the Vestibular Disorders Association says it's best to avoid anything high in sugar and salt, caffeine and alcohol, in order to help maintain the balance of fluids in the ears.

Always consult your professional healthcare providers before making any changes to your diet, or if you have concerns about your current health and nutritional intake.

Smell and Taste

When I was expecting my first child, I was able to smell anything sour from a mile away, especially vinegar. I knew if the food around me had even the faintest trace of vinegar. I was experiencing temporary hyperosmia — an oversensitivity to smell, which is common in pregnant women.

Even now, my husband comments I have a strong sense of smell. I believe it is why I enjoy food so much. I find food aromas very stimulating, in that they make me want to ingest and digest everything!

I plan to enjoy the smell and taste of food for as long as I can. Unfortunately, after the age of 50, the number of taste buds decreases and the membranes lining our nose become thinner and drier, so we lose some smell and taste. As a consequence, we find food more bland as we age.

I will always love the smell of freshly cut grass, the dry ground quenched by the rain, the ionic air before a thunderstorm and the saltiness of the sea breeze. Smelling all of these make me feel alive and very much connected to my environment.

The more connected I am, the better I intuit.

The Nose that Knows

It is incredible to consider how acute the senses of taste and smell are for food tasters and perfumers, respectively. I bet they are so intuitive in their job that they no longer need to see labels to figure out specific ingredients of food or perfume.

And then there's love. Did you know that pheromones attract a potential sexual partner and genetic match who is best suited to us for procreation and children-rearing? We smell them. We want them! They smell us. They want us!

Procreation is an instinctive biological process fundamental to survival.

Choosing a mate for companionship, pleasure, love, happiness and satisfaction (all aspects of a thriving life) is within the domain of intuition.

The process by which our smell influences our choice in a mate is sophisticated, and there are many aspects scientists still do not understand. A 'perfect match' means that there is enough genetic difference in the immune systems to complement what each partner possesses, making for stronger immunity for the offspring. Women taking contraceptive pills smell less attractive to men. According to *Smart Publications,* experts advise alternative contraception and avoiding products that mask our scents when getting to know a potential long-term partner. The fact that the nose has all this to say about mating smells like absolute magic!

I think the practice of using a lot of perfume nowadays has distracted and weakened our noses. Perhaps it is one of the reasons many relationships end in divorce — because we can't suitably sniff the natural odours of the right person to begin with. I sometimes wonder if it even relates to depression in some way. Because if we can hardly smell ourselves, would that be akin to losing our sense of self, which would adversely affect our thought processes? I truly believe this.

I also believe, as part of intuiting, that our noses can be trained to differentiate the smell between 'good' and 'bad' people. We need new research to support or disprove this, but recent studies by Dr Lilianne Mujica-Parodi, a cognitive neuroscientist at Stony Brook University in New York, have shown that we can distinguish different types of sweat, even on the unlaundered t-shirt of a stranger. Research subjects were able to sense whether the person wearing the shirt had sweat out of fear, or simply an intense workout.

A weak sense of smell can unquestionably affect our quality of life.

For four years, starting at the age of 12, my daughter suffered from nasal polyps and persistent sinusitis. During a recent dinner conversation, while we enjoyed the meal my husband cooked, she mentioned the period of time when she couldn't fully taste because she couldn't smell food properly. She could only distinguish sweet, acidic/sour, salty, or bitter, but not the aromatic and flavourful tastes and layers that make food enjoyable. She's 26 now with a healthy sense of smell, which makes her truly appreciate the yumminess of her meals.

Vitamin D, alpha-lipoic acid, vitamins A, B6, B12, zinc and copper all help maintain the extraordinary abilities of our nose.

Buddy Buds

Taste is an essential sense that we often take for granted with respect to its strong link to survival. Our taste can discriminate between that which is nutritious, tasty and enjoyable, and that which is potentially poisonous and fatal. We use our sense of taste everytime we eat or drink, the two most critical processes contributing to our well-being.

We have five known taste receptors, which are: sweet, salty, sour, bitter and umami (savoury). Scientists are currently debating over seven more contenders for a sixth official taste, including fat, metallicity, coolness (like menthol and peppermint), and piquance (spicy). Each sense of taste has a basis in our biological needs and is meant to protect and inform our bodes about the foods that we need to eat or avoid in order to survive.

(1) Sweet is primarily to distinguish which foods are high in energy. It is usually caused by natural and artificial sugars/sweeteners.

(2) Salty is to detect sodium in our body — vital to many bodily functions such as maintaining the balance of fluid in our body.

(3) Sour is to distinguish food that may be spoilt and rotten, or not suitable for consumption anymore.

(4) Bitter is to detect poison or toxins present in food, since most poisons are bitter. We have 25 bitter taste receptor genes working together to keep us safe.

(5) Umami is to identify protein-rich food.

It is important to note that not every bitter food or substance is poisonous. And not every sour food is rotten. Coffee, tea, alcohol, the bittermelon, and many other bitter vegetables are beneficial to our health, as are sour lemons and limes, kombucha, apple cider vinegar, and many pickled foods.

Our sense of taste for bitter and sweet, and partially for sour, is genetically inherited and comes with certain predispositions. Those who prefer sweet may have a tendency to become overweight, and they are more predisposed to metabolic syndrome, which is a group of health issues that increase the risk for serious health conditions like heart disease and diabetes.

By knowing our taste preferences, we can know more about our genetic inheritance. For instance, a mother who is naturally averse to broccoli could have an offspring who is also broccoli-averse. But plenty of exposure to the food early on in the child's development can decrease the aversion.

Bear in mind that taste changes as we age, and is considerably influenced by our experiences.

For some of us who have easy access to diverse food, especially carbohydrates and sweets, food addiction can be a problem.

I'm finding it hard to resist carbohydrates like rice because I grew up eating rice all the time. Exposure to diverse cultures that are gastronomically rich has left me with such a great appreciation — and cravings — for certain foods. Now that I've been living in New Zealand for a while, my taste for sweets has peaked. There are so many readily available cakes, pastries and other yummy desserts. If I listened more to my body as a whole and not just my taste buds, I know it would be best for me to lessen my ingestion and digestion of such food. And if there continues to be a significant gap between my food intake and physical activity, then my insatiable ability to taste and savour food will become a potential liability. But it's so hard to turn down foods that taste so good, isn't it?

How are your buddy buds? What are your challenges?

Folic acid, vitamins B3 and B12, thiamin, zinc, and copper help our taste buds stay in shape and give us gastronomical pleasure for a long time.

Skin and Touch

The skin is our largest organ. It is spread over two square metres (22 square feet) and serves as our protective covering from environmental elements. Our sense of touch includes external factors that come into contact with the skin, as well as internal sensory receptors found in our joints, muscles, blood vessels and internal organs. That's where the visceral sensations of a heartbeat, the expansion of our lungs, and hunger pangs come from.

Touch is more than skin-deep. The five million sensory nerve receptors on our skin transmit messages to our brain, which allows us to process and translate the information we sense from both external and internal sources. It means that we feel the hot external temperature of a radiant heater and the internal heat of our feverish body when we are sick.

I remember with each of my three pregnancies, I would often touch my tummy to feel the baby growing inside me. I couldn't help but think they also sensed it because suddenly there would be lots of movement and kicking. It was as if they were showing me their appreciation, which reassured me that everything would be alright.

When my kids were infants with colic, I rubbed their tummies gently. I know it soothed them because they would stop crying. They're all adults now, but I'm still a touchy-feely mom. I like hugging and kissing them every chance I get. I do this not just as a reminder of my love and affection for them, but also to shower them with something I did not get enough of while growing up.

I grew up on a tropical island where temperatures, which were always from the twenties to the high thirties in degrees Celsius (low seventies to triple digits in degrees Fahrenheit), were supposed to keep our bodies warm. It worked for most, but not entirely for me. I remember after every handshake, people would remark about my cold hands. My facial reaction would prompt some of them to say 'cold hands, warm heart', perhaps as an afterthought to how awkward they must have made me feel.

Later in life, I would find myself witness to a similar situation with someone else who had cold hands. It was when Daddy-O, my father-in-law, was rushed to the hospital. A doctor obviously needed to touch him to measure his pulse, temperature — the works. She was attentive, friendly and seemed to know what she was doing. Except she had cold hands. So as soon as Daddy-O felt her, he emphatically said, 'Your hands are cold! I would never marry someone with cold hands!'

She smiled back, unfazed, and continued to assess him. But I was thinking — cold hands or not, I bet, at the end of her hectic day, she would be longing for a caring touch and a relaxing massage to magically relieve her stress and soothe away her achy muscles, just like the rest of us.

When we feel the touch of a person we trust and love, it gives us warmth and comfort. When it comes from a stranger or a person we dislike, it can elicit a powerful reaction of being violated, and feel like an invasion of our personal space. We may experience anger and anxiety because we have not given the right and permission to touch us.

Touch of Hope

When I was twelve, I almost died.

It started out as a great Christmas holiday with my aunt, uncle and their university classmates. We tramped to this beautiful waterfall. It was so enchanting in my eyes, even as a child. Everybody braved the ice-cold water and jumped in to swim and have fun. I wanted to join in, but I didn't know how. So, we found some coconuts that I could use to keep me afloat. With the permission of the adults, once they had tested the coconuts' floatation-worthiness, I had a go at it. I was enjoying myself so much until suddenly I felt a downward pull.

I didn't understand what was going on. I struggled to stay afloat, but I was being dragged further down with my coconuts. I felt my life slowly ebbing away with the cold water invading my body. The last thought I had was the hope that I could feel the touch of someone and not die alone, or that some miracle pull me out of death's grip. The Universe heard me. I felt not just a touch, but a tug on my arm and the next thing I knew I was out of the water. My uncle saved me from a very strong undertow.

There are countless stories of people who lived through horrible accidents. They say that feeling the touch of another person in that critical moment — a rescuer, a paramedic, a helpful stranger or a fellow victim — was what a made the difference between life and death. That touch inspired a firm hold on to their will to survive.

When a person is dying, we believe and hope that by holding their hand, we can help them cross over more peacefully and contentedly, knowing that they are not alone. Touch is powerful in this way.

We take care of our sense of touch by caring for our skin, as well as all of the other sensory organs connected to it.

Here are some of the nutrients ideal for healthy touch: vitamins A, C, D and E, Omega-3 fatty acids, some proteins and lactobacilli.

Vitamin A is an antioxidant known to protect our skin from the ill effects of harmful UV rays. Vitamin C fights scurvy, and topical vitamin E reduces sunburned cells and UVB skin damage. Oral vitamin D treatment can prevent skin cancer and is known for its anti-ageing effects.

Muscles and Joints

Movement and an absence of pain are necessary to clear our mind and body and be open to intuition. We must keep our muscles and joints healthy. Calcium and magnesium complement each other to control cramps, regulate heartbeat, blood pressure, and cell reproduction, and reduce inflammation. Calcium is good for the overall health of our bones. Vitamin D helps our body absorb calcium more efficiently. An imbalance in the ratio of calcium and magnesium in the body result in diseases such as prostate cancer.

Blood Vessels

There are three major types of blood vessels: the arteries, veins, and capillaries. Amazingly, when placed end to end, they would stretch nearly 161,000 km (approximately 100,000 miles), enough to circle Earth nearly four times. Our blood vessels carry blood, which contains oxygen and nutrients, throughout our body — especially to and from our heart. Unhealthy blood vessels, such as those subject to cholesterol build-up, will significantly impact our heart, brain, and other organs, leading to serious disease and even death.

Omega-3 fatty acids are vital in making hormones that regulate blood clotting, contraction and relaxation of artery walls and inflammation. They keep the platelets healthy, which helps reduce the risk of heart disease and stroke. Vitamin B12 helps build red blood cells and maintains healthy nerves. Potassium helps lower blood pressure, while folic acid and vitamin B help form DNA and red blood cells.

Nutrition Guide

What follows is a comprehensive list of all of the vitamins and minerals mentioned, along with their benefits and food sources.

I recommend you do your own research about other foods that are good sources of essential nutrients for the brain and the body. *And remember: always consult your doctor before undergoing any diet changes or supplementation!*

Information about the best sources for each nutrient comes from the University of Maryland Medical Center, Dieticians of Canada, the American Pregnancy Association, and the New Zealand Nutrition Foundation.

OMEGA-3 FATTY ACIDS

Benefit:

— *brain* (improve cognition, reduces depression)

— *eyes* (prevent age-related macular degeneration and dry eye syndrome, reduce the risk of glaucoma, promote healthy tears and proper eye drainage)

— *blood vessels* (regulate blood clotting, contraction and relaxation of artery walls and inflammation, keep platelets healthy, reduce the risk of heart disease and stroke)

Sources:

- algae
- cod liver oil
- fish (salmon, tuna, halibut, mackerel, lake trout, herring sardines)
- flaxseed and flaxseed oils
- krill
- leafy green vegetables
- nuts (especially walnuts) and nut oils
- vegetable oils

VITAMIN A

Benefits:

— *eyes* (protects cornea)

— *nose*

— *skin* (protects from UV rays)

Sources:

- beef
- carrots
- chicken liver
- dairy products (whole milk, milk yoghurt, milk cottage cheese, butter, other cheeses)
- eggs
- fish liver oils
- mango
- papaya
- pumpkin
- sweet potato
- veal

VITAMIN B

Benefits:

— *blood vessels* (helps form DNA and red blood cells)

Sources:

- cheese
- eggs
- fish
- meat
- milk and milk products

* poultry
* shellfish

VITAMIN B1 (THIAMIN)

Benefits:

— *taste buds*

Sources:

* whole-grain or enriched cereals and rice
* legumes
* wheat germ
* bran
* brewer's yeast
* nuts
* blackstrap molasses
* pork
* beef
* poultry
* organ meats

VITAMIN B3 (NIACIN)

Benefits:

— *taste buds*

Sources:

* avocado
* green peas
* liver
* mushrooms
* peanuts

- poultry
- sunflower seeds
- tuna

VITAMIN B6

Benefits:

— *nose*

Sources:

- beans
- beans
- beef
- eggs
- fish
- fortified breakfast cereal
- nuts
- peas
- seafood
- seeds
- soy products
- turkey

VITAMIN B12

Benefits:

— *nose*

— *taste buds*

— *blood vessels* (build red blood cells, maintain healthy nerves)

Sources:

- cheese

- eggs

- fish

- fortified soy and rice beverages

- meat

- milk

- poultry

- shellfish

- soy-based meat substitutes

VITAMIN C

Benefits:

— *eyes* (with vitamin A: promotes healthy retinal capillaries and maintains healthy connective tissues like the collagen found in the cornea)

— *ears*

— *skin* (fights scurvy)

Sources:

- blueberries

- cabbage

- cantaloupe

- citrus fruits (oranges, grapefruit)

- cranberries

- kiwifruit

- leafy green vegetables

- lettuce

- mango

- papaya

- peppers

- pineapple
- potato
- raspberries
- strawberries
- tomato
- watermelon

VITAMIN D

Benefits:

— *nose*

— *skin* (anti-ageing, prevents skin cancer)

Sources:

- beef liver
- egg yolk
- fatty fish
- fortified foods such as milk, cereals and juices
- mushrooms
- sunlight
- supplements

VITAMIN E

Benefits:

— *eyes* (with vitamin A: decreases risk of age-related macular degeneration),

— *ears*

— *skin* (topical cream reduces UVB skin damage)

Sources:

- avocado

* canola oil

* corn oil

* leafy greens such as kale

* nuts

* safflower oil

* seeds

* some types of margarine

* soybean oil

* sunflower oil

* wheat germ

ALPHA-LIPOIC ACID

Benefits:

— *nose*

Sources:

* broccoli

* Brussels sprouts

* organ meats (heart, liver, kidneys)

* peas

* spinach

* supplementation

* tomato

* yeast

BETA-CAROTENE

Benefits:

— *eyes* (with vitamin A: decreases risk of age-related macular degeneration)

— *ears*

Sources:

- broccoli
- cantaloupe
- carrots
- leafy green vegetables
- lettuce
- spinach
- sweet potato
- tomato
- winter squash

CALCIUM

Benefits:

— *muscles and joints* (controls cramps, reduce inflammation, regulate heartbeat. blood pressure, and cell reproduction, good for bone health)

Sources:

- collards
- fortified foods such as orange juice, oatmeal and breakfast cereal
- kale
- okra
- perch
- rainbow trout
- salmon
- sardines
- soybeans
- spinach

- white beans

COPPER

Benefits:

— *eyes*

— *nose*

— *taste buds*

Sources:

- almonds
- asparagus
- avocado
- beef liver
- dark chocolate
- dried apricots
- lentils
- miso
- molasses
- mushrooms
- prunes
- seafood
- sunflower seeds

FOLATE/FOLIC ACID

Benefits:

— *brain* (prevents cognitive decline and dementia)

— *taste buds*

— *blood vessels* (helps form DNA and red blood cells)

Sources:

- beans
- beans
- bread
- cereal
- chickpeas
- citrus fruits
- dark green vegetables
- lentils
- pasta
- rice
- spinach
- supplements

LACTOBACILLI

Benefits:

— *skin*

Sources:

- fermented cabbage
- kimchi
- pickled vegetables
- sauerkraut
- yoghurt

MAGNESIUM

Benefits:

— *ears*

— *muscles and joints* (control cramps, reduce inflammation, regulate heartbeat. blood pressure, and cell reproduction)

Sources:

- almonds
- avocado
- banana
- black beans
- chard
- dark chocolate
- pumpkin seeds
- spinach
- yoghurt or kefir

POTASSIUM

Benefits:

— *blood vessels* (lowers blood pressure)

Sources:

- acorn squash
- avocado
- coconut water
- dried apricot
- pomegranate
- spinach
- sweet potato
- wild-caught salmon

ZINC

Benefits:

— *eyes* (with vitamin A: decreases risk of age-related macular degeneration)

— *nose*

— *taste buds*

Sources:

- cheese (ricotta, Swiss, gouda)
- crab
- oysters
- poultry
- red meat
- shellfish
- shrimp

Exercise

From an early age, I learned that exercise matters. In my grade school years, after the flag ceremony and the Pledge of Allegiance, we had around 15–30 minutes of callisthenics before heading off to our classroom for our first class. In secondary school, we had physical education focused on exercise, dance and sports.

When I was raising my kids in Manila, it was hot and humid, and air pollution was a serious health hazard. Going to the mall with my three children, with four years and three years between them, was the next best alternative to burning calories. I had to keep up with their curiosity and running around, and it was great exercise. Cleaning and tidying up the house was exercise too. Everything was done manually such as washing the dishes, cooking, scrubbing the floor with a coconut husk until it was shiny, washing, hanging and ironing the clothes, and picking up the toys all over the house. Then there was less exercise when we bought our first washing machine and spin dryer.

With the modern-day convenience of electronics and household appliances, we exert less and less effort in keeping our houses clean and orderly. Spending a third of our day, at the least, sitting in front of the computer at work makes things worse exercise-wise.

I tried walking some years back which I enjoyed but found lonely since I walked on my own every time. Going to the gym to row and run on the treadmill was also good for a while, but then I got bored. For me, when exercise is rigidly regimented it never works in the long-term. It might work for a while, but it's not sustainable. I've noticed that keeping active with daily chores, walking, dancing to music I like, and just moving around has always worked best for me.

However, watching videos online of active women in their seventies, eighties and nineties weight-training and doing yoga has inspired me lately. I haven't tried either yet, so I'm looking forward to giving both a shot. I can't give up on finding physical fitness that works for me, most especially because of my predispositions.

Exercise keeps our body healthy and delays the physical ageing process and the mental decline associated with it. In fact, it enhances learning and memory by stimulating the growth of new neurons in our brain. It is also the best antidote to an unhealthy diet, particularly against sweets and unhealthy fats. Yet as much as we know we should, many of us struggle to incorporate exercise into our daily routine. And that includes me.

Studies show that our human ancestors were very aerobically active in their hunter-gatherer lifestyle, which allowed our species to evolve to live longer compared to other primates. Being sedentary contributes to many modern illnesses, including Alzheimer's and other age-related diseases. All of us have a gene called APOE. It tells us our likelihood of getting Alzheimer's. About 70% of the population has APOE3, which relates to a neutral risk. Another 5–10% have APOE2, indicating a reduced risk, and 10–15% have APOE4. People with APOE4 are predisposed to have a higher risk of Alzheimer's. Genetic testing can tell you which gene you have. If you have APOE4, exercise and managing hypertension are very important, and your degree of physical activity is what keeps this predisposition in check. The less active you are, the likelier you will suffer.

Researchers from the University of Canberra performed a variety of brain tests, to check the brain function of adults. They found that aerobic exercise improves cognitive abilities such as thinking, reading, learning and reasoning, while muscle training such as lifting weights had significant effects on the brain's memory, planning and organisation. Knowing this is a good starting point for us, so that we identify which kinds of exercises to do.

Aerobics and strength training are both essential to keep our brain's executive functions sharp.

Our ancestors did both types of exercise: long-distance walking to find food, and strength training to carry whatever they had hunted or gathered back home. In modern-day life, we can easily incorporate this by walking either to or from work.

I feel pretty blessed that I live near town, and it takes me an hour to walk home from work. It's around 4 km (2 ½ miles) each way. I would like to try to walk to work as well, and do both ways at least three times a week, realistically, but I haven't yet. If I wished to be even more ambitious, I'd carry both my bags while walking as part of my strength training five days a week. I'm sure it would make me fit and healthy, both mentally and physically, which makes a lot of sense. If you'd like to follow me on my public social media profiles, I'll be sure to keep you updated on my progress.

We need to start early and maintain regular activity to keep both our body and brain healthy well into our golden years and beyond.

According to a study by Dr Denise Park of the University of Texas at Dallas, learning new skills can ward off age-related mental disorders such as Alzheimer's and dementia. Quilting and digital photography were among the activities some of the 221 participants, aged 60–90 years old, decided to learn. Park found that maintaining social interaction and practising everyday skills such as crossword puzzles and sudoku had sound effects on the anti-ageing process, but not as significant as learning a new skill.

In her TED Talk 'The Benefits of a Bilingual Brain', Mia Nacamulli said that engaging in a second language leads to more activity in specific brain regions, delaying the onset of diseases like Alzheimer's and dementia by as much as five years. And an Edinburgh University study of 853 research participants showed that knowing another language is beneficial even when learned in adulthood.

Researchers at Penn State University found similar results in 39 participants of varying ages. Half of them took language lessons for six weeks, while the other half did not. They discovered that those who were able to learn a second language had more integrated and connected brain networks, and actually changed the brain both functionally and structurally. The extent of the changes varied according to age and other individual differences, but overall, the study showed that learning a second language can benefit the brain regardless of age and that we can train and shape our brain well into adulthood.

Sleep

Sleep is paramount to our brain's health. Our brain cradles our mind, and our mind is the seat of our essence that holds the memories that form our identity. Memory binds all the elements that form intuition, as examined in ZIQ1 and ZIQ2. Hence, sleep is essential to keeping our brains healthy and receptive to developing, advancing and sharpening intuition.

Sleep refines and improves the skills we learn during the day. It is while we are inactive during sleep that our body restores itself by growing muscles; repairing tissue, organs and bones; regenerating and replenishing proteins; and releasing growth hormone in developing children.

Sleep impacts our thought processes such as perception and the clarity required for decision-making. In fact, continuous sleep deprivation skews our perception, memories and behaviour towards negativity. No wonder some of us may be grumpy, overly sensitive, or unpleasant when we lack sleep.

A minimum of seven hours of sleep every night is vital to our overall well-being and positivity.

A complete sleep cycle composed of both NREM (non-rapid eye movement) and REM (rapid eye movement) sleep is critical in processing emotions during our sleep.

NREM sleep ranges from just falling asleep through a period of deep slow wave sleep. It occurs in three stages, from the beginning of the sleep cycle through very deep sleep. Each NREM cycle lasts between 90–120 minutes. Memories at this sleep stage appear to be compressed, played in small fragmented and accelerated bursts which serve to refine them to be better and more useful so that when we encounter similar situations in the future, we have already processed a way to improve our responses.

REM sleep usually occurs around 90 minutes after falling asleep. Experts say our memories are replayed in real-time at this stage. They speculate that REM sleep gives us the opportunity to relive our memories in order to move us into the future. In effect, it provides us with a space to test and learn whatever lessons we need to focus on without the same risk in our waking world. Hence, it is thought to be the key to creativity.

We'll also talk about the dreams produced during NREM and REM sleep in Chapter 6: Intuition Tools — Dreams.

It seems to me that when we are awake, our neurons talk to each other in a very controlled manner. When we are asleep, they communicate without interference or directives from our conscious thoughts, making them active and creative in connecting the dots when processing memories.

While awake, our neurons seem to be functioning on a leash per se, following commands and doing what they are told. But while asleep, they function with free rein — they become directors, artists, philosophers, geniuses and brilliant scientists inventors or problem solvers. Hence, it is essential to give our neurons the freedom of a full night's sleep for the good of our brain health, creativity and intuition.

I have always loved sleep. When I was younger, up until my early thirties, I would sleep in every chance I got. Eight to ten hours of sleep was usual for me. It somehow healthfully influenced my appetite, because I only ate when I was hungry. My cravings for sweets were nearly nonexistent. I picked up and learned new things quickly. I worked fast and efficiently and seldom had brain fog.

However, having said this, I also have a history of insomnia dating as far back as I can remember. There would be times when I would stay awake most of the night, just starting to get drowsy around four in the morning. It was a big problem since I had to be at school by seven. On those days, I would be forced to function all the day long on only about an hour's worth of sleep. I would find myself struggling to keep my eyes open during lectures. So I would look forward to getting home to sleep early by six o'clock. The only problem was that then I would wake up again by midnight, and the cycle of sleep deprivation would continue.

In hindsight, during my depression in my early thirties, I remember barely sleeping at all. It's not that I didn't want to sleep, but I just couldn't because of insomnia. It was a catch-22 sort of thing, or 'Which comes first, the chicken or the egg?' Did my sleep deprivation cause my depression or did my depression cause my sleep deprivation? It was probably both, and they fed off of each other. Perhaps having low-energy and lacking essential nutrients triggered my depression, which in turn aggravated my insomnia.

A recent sleep study called 'The Triad Study', led by Dr Jack D Edinger, examined patients with both depression and insomnia. Results from the study showed that seven hours or more of sleep a night was the most effective method to mitigate depression, with a 62.5% remission rate among patients sleeping at least that long.

Sleep is important.

I remember one crazy work project when I was in my mid-thirties when I worked in front of my computer for four days straight with barely any sleep. The most I got was a four-hour nap, spread over four days. That was very dangerous.

Recently, I've heard stories about gamers who take not sleeping to a whole new level. A couple years back, a 32-year-old Taiwanese man died after gaming for three days straight.

Staying awake to the death might be an extreme case, but prolonged sleep deprivation can lead to a heightened risk of heart disease, kidney disease, high blood pressure, diabetes, stroke and a vulnerable immune system, and can even trigger the brain to eat itself. Researchers at the Marche Polytechnic University in Italy found that 'a lack of sleep can cause parts the brain's synapses to be "eaten" by other brain cells', according to several news articles written in May 2017.

I would have never risked being sleep deprived had I known then what I know now!

As I have gotten older, I'm lucky enough if I get around five to six hours of sleep. My appetite for sweets has increased considerably. I eat more than I need, out of habit or boredom. It is no wonder I have gained 12 kilograms (about 26 ½ pounds) in the last decade. Perhaps it is a combination of many other things, including a hormonal imbalance from perimenopause, but I'm sure that my sleep has something to do with it.

My lack of sleep for prolonged periods has resulted in frequent brain fogs, as well. These days, whenever I lack sleep for consecutive nights, the third night means a complete loss of productivity the next day, not to mention the barely productive days from the prior nights of inadequate sleep. My continuous lack of sleep can snowball into an inability to think, analyse and write. On some occasions, I choose not to book appointments with clients, because I know it will only be counterproductive.

I am a poster child for proving that lack of sleep makes us susceptible to a lot of problems. I've experienced depression, weight gain (which can lead to obesity), brain fog, and all the complications and consequences that go along with those issues, thanks to sleep problems.

The more I appreciate the inner workings of intuition, the more I realise how my total well-being correlates to it. Prolonged sleep deprivation puts us in the survival mode which is the domain of instinct, not intuition.

The only way to intuit is to take care of our physical and mental needs. Then we can be open to possibility.

We absolutely must take care of ourselves. Otherwise, something's going to give.

To get back the critical time necessary for our brain to clean and heal itself, and process the memories of our experiences with all the emotions attached to them, we need to sleep.

That is why the following proverb rings as true today as it always has: 'Early to bed, early to rise, makes a person healthy, wealthy, and wise.'

Part 4: Developing Intuition

Chapter 5   Thinking Methods

Timing is Everything

I believe my Lola Mommy was ahead of her time in so many ways, including her tips on how I could learn better. She instilled in me the value of education and a learner's mindset at a young age.

I remember her telling me that instead of cramming to study for an exam for several days, day and night, I could spend less time immediately before the exam preparing (as much or as little time as I felt I needed to feel ready). But there was a catch. To avoid cramming meant I would have to make studying a habit. Studying meant reviewing what I had learned each day by mentally reviewing the lectures, and comparing my memory to my notes — including thinking about and looking over the things I did not yet understand. She said that I should make studying and reviewing a consistent routine, every night, before I went to sleep, all throughout the school year. She even told me to put the book or my notes under my pillow when I end my nightly review ritual, and literally 'sleep on it'. This way, I would remember what I had studied the previous night when I woke up.

She was teaching me then what experts and researchers show us today. The best time to learn is before sleep. Our brains file, organise, and consolidate the last thing we think about during our waking hours first, and subsequently the lessons we learned during the day.

There's no evidence to support her advice to place my book under the pillow, but I always thought — and I still think — the idea was a clever and appropriate gesture to condition my brain to prioritise processing and sorting the particular contents that I reviewed before I slept.

It's fantastic how Lola Mommy taught me in a very common sense style. There was no internet in the '70s, no readily available research papers where she could have gotten this idea. Could it be that Lola Mommy's *intuition* was the source of this knowledge? She knew it would work, without knowing the precise details of how it works, or what makes it work. She just knew.

Of course, we have to use our own common sense to know our schedules and find the time that works best for whatever we need to do in our lives. First priority: When do we go to bed? Reviewing material way past bedtime, until exhaustion sets in, is self-defeating. We need to recognise when our bodies say that we need to sleep, and we need to respect this.

If we are usually off to bed by 11pm, then we need to integrate a schedule which would allow for our review ritual a half an hour to an hour before bedtime.

Listen to your body and do not go beyond a period where you just feel stretched too thin, spent, stressed or forced. A functional headspace is key if you plan to review before you sleep.

When you're ready, review the skills you want to improve upon, based on your memories of the day. Review but do not obsess. Just KISS. (In my family, we take KISS to mean, 'keep it short and straightforward'. Not the more demeaning 'keep it simple, stupid' that may come to mind for some of you.)

Let's say your goal is to strengthen your intuition and deepen your understanding of the research and stories in this book. In that case, you would review the lessons you read, and think about how intuition presented itself in your day today.

Be disciplined about doing this every night. It is through practice and repetition that we are able to rewire and restructure our brain to acquire new skills or functions. Repetition is how we create new neural connections to facilitate long-term learning and retention.

There is no shortcut, no magic pill.

Our brain is malleable and ever-changing, according to the direction we want to develop or shape it, but we need to be consistent. Our development rates vary from one person to the next. Some of us take more time, and some take less. The pace we find comfortable is a personal choice.

In the process of your nightly review, start off with ZIQ1 and ZIQ2 as your guide to prompt a better understanding of yourself. Remember, everyday behaviour and practice are pivotal. Habit, habit, habit.

Memory and Imagination

We have established that the best time to review and retain what we learn is before sleep.

What should we review, and how do we do it? This is where memory and imagination come in.

Kids have a vivid imagination, which is critical to their developing brain. They use it all the time, especially when playing. In their minds, they can create different kinds of worlds, scenarios, tools, characters, and storylines — whatever they need to fill in the gaps. If we ask them what they imagine, we would be surprised at how strikingly and excitingly they can describe something that exists in their minds.

Much of what they imagine is rooted in things they might have seen — like a show, a picture, a place visited, a comic superhero character, a story heard, or a book read.

Memory is the seed that inspires imagination.

It's a bit sad that in adulthood some of us forget how powerful imagination is. We underestimate it and take it for granted. Those who have harnessed and consistently used it have become creative and innovative enough to change the world. Look at Bill Gates, Steve Jobs, Larry Page and Sergey Brin. We are very dependent on the technologies they have imagined and created.

We can be quite imaginative beings. At its best, imagination allows us to create art, literature, business, music, and ultimately attain our goals.

At its worst, imagination cripples us. We invent things in our minds that scare or worry us to death — crimes, personal loss, failure, all sorts things that may not (yet) exist.

Let us instead reframe how this works by imagining exciting practicable stuff that we can use to our advantage.

The Right Way to Worry

As much as we would love never to worry, we do. It's human nature. So, instead of scaring or worrying ourselves to death and doing nothing about it, let's rewire our brains by changing the way we worry.

We must respond to our worries only if we can equally imagine practical solutions — the many options and scenarios that challenge, address and resolve our worries. In this way, healthy worrying can evolve into the gift of foresight.

Of course, we can never change the past, but we can use our memories to create better future memories through the imagination. When we recognise things we could have done differently, we can start to change our future behaviour. How?

(1) Imagine the many better ways we could respond.

(2) Evaluate those responses.

(3) Prepare and work toward a better outcome the next time we encounter a similar situation.

This method gives us an uncomplicated formula of *better = better*, where *better responses yield better outcomes*.

Here's what I usually do when I worry, using a process that involves both memory and imagination.

1. I identify my worry.

2. I challenge my worry so I can recognise if it is based on experience (memory) or imagined.

3. If based on experience, then I have to remember how and what I did in response and whether I was successful or not so I can think of other ways to make better outcomes that give me options.

4. If imagined, meaning it is something entirely new where I lack experience, then I need to recognise the nature of the situation, people, resources required, time required and other 'whats and hows' that can place me in a better position for a better outcome. Remember *better = better* as a guideline is a solid foundation for any plan.

5. If worry is imagined but triggered by memory, then I go back to No. 3.

6. If worry is neither from memory nor anticipation of a new experience, then I try my best to recognise its source and examine that relationship. If I cannot identify or validate the source of the worry, then this type of worry is just a waste of time. I don't want to spend any of my precious brain resources this way.

Some might argue that worry is our intuition telling us something out of the blue. But it's not. Intuition is about knowing.

If it were intuition, we wouldn't worry at all, because we would *know* it, even if we didn't *know how we knew*, and our mind would already be working out its response.

Regardless of the outcome, by framing our worries in this practical manner, we learn many alternative ways to adequately address what we fear. By using our imagination as a practice place to try out different options and strategies, we bring about better results in real-life situations.

Every time we imagine the outcome we want, we add to our memory of knowledge. Through practice and mastery, we rewire our brain to use worrying as a means of stimulating *instinctive insight*. In other words: *intuition*.

The Triunity Approach

The Triunity Approach is the structure in which to practice our new 'right way to worry' thinking method.

We often hear the saying 'there are two sides of the same coin'. It is consistent with the duality around us:

  — the positive and the negative polarities;

  — the sun and the moon (day and night);

  — the magnetic fields (north and south);

  — culture (primarily East and West);

  — philosophical/spiritual beliefs (yin and yang, light and dark, good and evil);

  — our mortality and transience (life and death).

It's similar to our way of thinking which is usually focused on good or bad, easy or difficult, win or lose, and other related thought processes.

To facilitate intuition, we have to rewire our brain by practising a thinking method that honours this universal duality by working with them both.

When we do this, we see not just a couple of trees in the forest but the forest itself, so to speak.

When we work with both parts of duality — optimism and pessimism, for example — we give each the opportunity to present us with everything they encompass. Boundaries and dependencies. Weaknesses and strengths. Risks and comfort zones. And so on. All these we could use to build an understanding that is more clear, more thorough, and multidimensional.

It is best to accept and work with our natural tendencies in our thought processes because going against what comes naturally is a complete waste of time and energy.

If we are natural worriers, we can indulge in worrying anytime. Provided we act and do something about it.

If our thoughts tend to focus more on the negative, we must also look at the positive.

We always need to work with both aspects of duality or not at all.

For what good will it do us if we are all for optimism, but we're oblivious to threats, obstacles, setbacks, or failure? It makes us vulnerable.

At the same token, what bad will it do if we are all for pessimism, but oblivious to peace, goodwill, perseverance, or success? It makes us unfortunate.

Either way, it's a disadvantage. Creating a workable area provides us with a fuller and more in-depth grasp of the scope and influences of this universal duality on our thought processes and decision-making.

Positive + Negative = Workable Area

Harmonising the positive and negative creates a space for balance and heightened awareness that presents an understanding that is neither ideal nor cynical, but practical and solid. This is the workable area. It provides us with the level-headedness to consider what the positive and the negative can give us — or not. It shows us the dependencies and complexities of both sides that can lead us to our next step.

The workable area prepares us for both success and failure by keeping us well-grounded and ready to bounce back either way. It gives us both the courage and the awareness of risks to be adventurous, and the humility and confidence — a powerful combination of virtues, best suited to successful interactions with others.

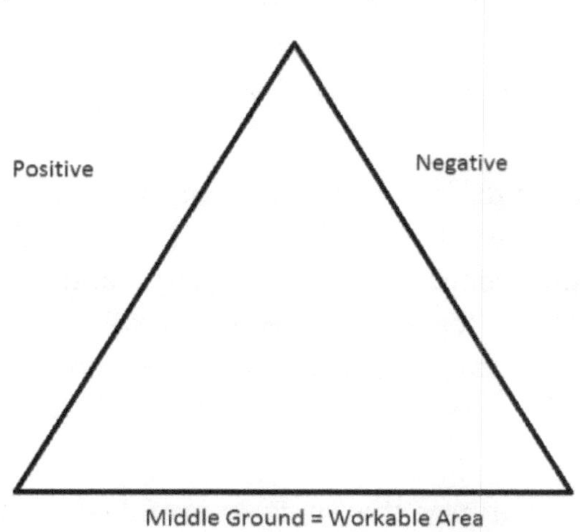

Figure 8. Triunity Approach = Workable Area

Here's how my thought process flows using the Triunity Approach.

I. Negative

What's the worst that can happen?

What or who can make this happen?

What can I do when it happens?

How can I stop this from happening?

II. Positive

What's the best thing that can happen?

What or who can make this happen?

What can I do when it doesn't happen?

How can I make this happen?

III. Workable Area: Action Plan and Solution

The answers to these questions will help me plan, prepare, review, imagine, and do.

I used to travel more often when I was younger. I remember how brave I was. I was also more adventurous, confident, street-smart, and I practised common sense for safety, which enabled me to visit countries that can be challenging for a woman travelling solo.

I now live in a city that it is peaceful and considered safe. I can mindlessly drop my purse somewhere and get a call from either the police lost-and-found or the person who picked it up off the street. I can walk everywhere without fear of being robbed or mugged. I'm grateful for this, and I wouldn't want to change anything. However, since I've been living here for years, I have turned soft, anxious and fearful of the idea of travelling alone.

Two years ago, I made arrangements to go to Paris and Amsterdam on my own. I read many online travel forums, where travellers talked a lot about becoming victims to pickpockets and thieves in both places. It made me very anxious.

I challenged my anxiety using the Triunity Approach to hopefully regain my confidence to travel alone. I found it beneficial since I was able to equally engage the unpleasant and the beautiful things that could potentially happen during the trip. This duality gave me the awareness necessary to create a workable space where I outlined my plans, contingencies, itinerary, safety measures and assessed the resources I would need to make my travel a memorable experience.

The months of preparation (that included the *timing is everything* thinking method of reviewing and imagining my travel plans before I slept) paid off. By the time I travelled, my intuition had kicked in. I was able to recognise whether a situation felt right or wrong, which kept me safe.

My travels were a success, and they also reawakened the wanderlust and confidence in me! I'm now planning my next big trip to either go around the world for the second time or to Eastern Europe as a golden birthday gift to myself. At the top of my itinerary wishlist are Scandinavia and the Baltics. (Any of you readers who live there, feel free to connect with me and let me know what I should see and do!)

Here's how my solo travel thought process flows using the Triunity Approach.

I. Negative: Unpleasant Experiences

What's the worst that can happen?

What or who can make this happen?

What can I do if it happens?

How can I stop this from happening?

II. Positive: Beautiful Opportunities

What's the best thing that can happen?

What or who can make this happen?

What can I do instead if it doesn't happen?

How can I make this happen?

III. Workable Area: Itinerary

The answers to these questions will help me plan, prepare, review, imagine, and do.

Past + Future = Present

The present and future are fluid and malleable, and even the past can change.

When we allow the past to conquer our mind and heart, we can become trapped with many unpleasant thoughts and feelings that are more likely to leave us enduringly heartbroken, jaded, angry, bitter, and generally invalidated.

I do not mean that we should disregard or bury the bad things in our past. On the contrary. We remember, but only to learn, to avoid repeating the same patterns, and to measure how far we have come.

The past is the best teacher.

It holds many snippets of wisdom and old maps that lead to many places like pinnacles, joys, heartaches, and failures. It keeps treasures of cherished memories that bind intuition, including the sensations and the deep emotions from some of our experiences.

Some of us live in the future and proudly call ourself dreamers.

However, *living in a dream* is different from *living for the dream*.

Living in a dream signifies denying and escaping the present, which could eventuate in living a nightmare if left uninterrupted.

Living for the dream means living in the present and using it as a blueprint to build our future.

When living for the dream, we give ourselves the opportunity to set new standards, have new experiences and adventures, face and overcome new challenges, and expand our horizons. As a consequence, we allow our perceptions across time — looking forward and backward — to evolve. What seemed too painful a year ago might appear to be a lifesaver in five years time. What we pined for four years ago might seem less significant next year. What we were afraid of yesterday might be the catalyst we need today to spur courage and bring forth achievements in the next five years.

Living in the *present*, with the vision of the *future* and the lessons of the *past*, is an incredible gift when we translate our timeline into purposeful actions.

Combined, they provide us with guidance and direction:

(1) first in our mind, through thoughts, imagination and dreams at night, and

(2) then in the realities of living every day and every moment, realistically creating each block needed to

(3) fulfil our goals.

Living in the present gives us the ability and opportunity to create our future, and to a degree, also change our past.

Here's how I process *Past + Future = Present* using the Triunity Approach.

I. Past

1. What happened?
2. What or who made it happen?
3. What did I do to make it happen?
4. What could have I done to stop it from happening?

II. Future

1. What do I want to happen?
2. What or who can make this happen?
3. What can I do if it doesn't happen?
4. How can I make this happen?

III. Workable Area: Present

The answers to these questions will help me recognise thoughts and patterns, hold myself accountable, plan, prepare, review, imagine, take responsibility, and build.

Triple Perspective = Me + S/He/They = Us

If we are directly involved with a person or a group and we don't know their perspective about something that impacts us both, then we don't have the complete picture. We need to know. We need the complete picture.

It's not unusual to have different perspectives and interests in situations that involve more than one person and require decision-making. We may experience tension or even clashes. For this reason, we need to appreciate all angles, including the breadth and depth of the issue — not to concede, but to find a workable area, if and when necessary.

It is a highly valued skill to connect and work with others when there is disharmony. It is an even more valued skill to create harmony where there is chaos.

Sometimes all it takes is a genuine interest in knowing what all parties want. Perhaps each party has complementary strengths and weaknesses and wants to handle tasks that match their skill set. Say, for example, one business partner is more introverted and wants to create products and set up systems, while the other is extroverted and wishes to handle sales and promotions. That can lead to an ideal team cooperating to achieve the whole — with continued communication, of course. Other times, there will be more deliberations and compromises to find the best solution for all parties involved.

Yet, 'we will never know unless we give it a go', as my husband often tells me. This is why we should make it our business to know.

If we want the same thing, then we can equally share the energy, responsibilities and resources required to produce or create the intended outcome. Ideally, it will make the work enjoyable and quicker to complete.

If, however, the vision is not shared, and either party isn't willing to compromise, or if neither is, then conflict and failure are likely. Flexibility and openness to a change in strategy are deemed wise and advantageous. If you find yourself in this situation, consider finding someone else who shares your vision and values, and is willing to work together amidst the different styles and approaches.

Here's how I process *Triple Perspective* using the Triunity Approach.

I. Me
1. What do I want?
2. Why do I want it?
3. Who else wants it?
4. What can I do to make it happen?
5. What can s/he/they contribute to making it happen?
6. How can we work together?
7. What can I do if it doesn't happen?

II. S/He/They
1. What do they want?
2. Why do they want it?
3. Who else wants what they want?
4. What can they do to make it happen?
5. What can the others contribute to making it happen?
6. How can we work together?
7. What can they do if it doesn't happen?

III. Workable Area: Us

The answers to these questions will help us recognise shared and differing values and visions, establish accountability, plan, prepare, review, imagine, share responsibility, communicate, and build.

Multidirectional, Multidimensional Thinking

Travel expands our mind as it exposes us to different peoples and ways of doing things. Everywhere we go, different cultures and perspectives exist. At the same token, we take our own with us wherever we go.

Our environment influences and experiences us as much as we influence and experience it.

Experiencing is the best way to learn about both the inner and outer workings of our world and give our minds the opportunity to expand.

When our mind expands, it becomes better equipped to hold the enlightenment and richness that diversity offers to foster intuition.

Let's look into the four key aspects of multidirectional, multidimensional thinking:

(1) Understanding and Appreciating Diversity,

(2) The Centre,

(3) Removing the Blinders, and

(4) Peripheral Vision and the Sidelights.

Understanding and Appreciating Diversity

There's no other way to sharpen our intuition except by having a good understanding and appreciation of diversity — in humanity and in nature. That's why it's wise to focus in on its cultural and individual aspects.

Diversity opens up our eyes, hearts and minds to the realities of what it means to be part of this world. It presents us with the truth about how the many cultural similarities and differences between us become either more pronounced or dimmed at the individual level.

Cultural diversity cannot just be described as either Eastern or Western. It also has northern and southern aspects, further parsed into national and regional identities, rural and urban environments, neighbourhoods, religious and philosophical beliefs, and even family ties and friendships. Each level layers on unique aspects to who we are, how we think, and how we intuit.

For instance, the Philippines is situated in Southeast Asia. It is comprised of 7,107 islands. The 100+ million population is more or less geographically split along religious lines:

— The Christian majority, at 92% of the population, lives in the northern and central parts of the country, on the main island of Luzon and in the Visayas.

— The Muslim minority, at 5.5% of the population, lives down south on the island of Mindanao.

This significant difference in culture and beliefs, exacerbated by the geographic divide and the wide statistical variance, has always been a source of contention in the Philippines. It is the reason some people of Mindanao are separatist.

Returning to our thought processes and perspectives, looking at things as one-dimensional — Eastern or Western — provides us with only a fraction of a point of view. That can be limiting and lead to invalid conclusions. We need to extend our considerations beyond that which immediately meets the eye, and examine multiple layers and dimensions. Sticking with geography, we would also look at Northern or Southern, urban or rural, valley or mountain, desert or rainforest, etc. The more layers we have, the more comprehensive our understanding.

Extra depth is good. By learning how to see things multidimensionally, we are able to peel the layers until we uncover the truth.

A multidimensional perspective weans us from stereotyping and generalising, which is far too prevalent these days. It may seem obvious, but: Just because we met a nasty person from a particular country doesn't mean everyone from that country is the same.

We block intuition when we think that any singular aspect of a person's identity —their ethnicity, religion, or economic circumstances — says everything we need to know about them.

Respect for individual diversity is critical. It gives us the opportunity to know a person through their views and experiences of the world, which can be indicative of their personality, values, thought processes, sentiments, and aspirations. We can then better appreciate our similarities and differences and recognise our shared humanity.

Knowledge is the root of all communication. It is the expression and recognition of how and who we are in the eyes of others and vice versa. It baffles me why most of us ignore this, considering we are highly social beings wired to learn from interacting with countless people throughout our lifetime — unless we live in isolation either by choice or circumstance.

The Centre

The breadth and depth of our understanding evolve when we practice multidirectional thinking, strengthening our intuition as a result. By observing and considering all possible thinking directions, we define where balance and harmony start. This represents our centre or workable area in the Triunity Approach.

Our centre is where we stand with conviction. It is our current reference point that shows how near or far off the mark we are with regards to the path we are heading down or considering. Having a centre means finding what works for ourselves, and the point of compromise we would accept to achieve cooperation when dealing with others.

Our centre identifies our comfort zone and its boundaries, which may be manifested as limitations — or 'points of no return' — when pursuing new experiences or endeavours. They can also manifest as fears that drive us to reject change. Sometimes our centre falls upon a perspective that is obvious and rings true, even if it feels uncomfortable.

Our centre empowers us with:

(1) courage, every time we venture away from it, and

(2) progress, when we cross our thresholds and boundaries.

Yet, it also reassures us with a familiarity we can always revisit if we ever need to pause to find our bearing and gather our strength.

Here's the flow of how I practice Multidirectional, Multidimensional Thinking using the Triunity Approach. It's the same flow when determining the workable area. The only difference is that we're focusing on diversity, which comes in many forms – varying perspectives, social dynamics, culture, personal preferences, politics, schools of thought, and others that would require the centre in order to find balance, and see the big picture.

I consider:

(1) the positive mix, and

(2) the negative mix

of each thinking direction, with

(3) the centre representing the workable area signifying

(4) a better understanding.

Culture
East (positive + negative)
+ West (positive + negative)
= Centre (understanding)

North (positive + negative)
+ South (positive + negative)
= Centre (understanding)

Politics
Left (positive + negative)
+ Right (positive + negative)
= Centre (understanding)

School of Thought
Forwards or Progressive (positive + negative)
+ Backwards or Regressive (positive + negative)
= Centre (understanding)

Personal Preference and Social Dynamics
Above or Transcendence (positive + negative)
+ Below or Failure and Mediocrity (positive + negative)
= Centre (understanding)

Removing the Blinders

Merriam-Webster Dictionary defines blinders as 'a limitation or obstruction to sight or discernment'. The term comes from the accessory known as a blinder, which was a flap on a horse's bridle to keep it from seeing peripheral objects.

With respect to intuition, I would define blinders as anything (good or bad) that could cloud our judgement. Some examples would be denial, escapism, weakness, fears, anxieties, trauma, hopes, emotional attachments, desire, passion, happiness, attraction, and so on.

Our blinders are personal, usually influenced by our environment and experiences.

We wear blinders to some degree every day. They may contribute to a lapse in judgement. Blinders can make us closed, unreceptive, unreasonably stubborn, and rigid. With them on, we suffer from a lack of foresight. We become deliberately selective of our perspective and operate without an appreciation of the bigger picture.

On other occasions, we place ourselves in the company of the wrong people and can end up compromising our values and principles. Not just once, but over and over again. A repetitive pattern of behaviour — a habit — forms and cripples our discernment.

Sometimes we wear our blinders to protect ourselves from something or someone that might cause us upset, hurt, or (God forbid) guilt! At times like this, we think that 'ignorance is bliss' and what we don't know won't hurt us. We're wrong.

For similar reasons, our blinders could also represent a 'No-Go Zone' — a deliberate choice to limit ourselves, and remain incompetent to some degree, either unconsciously or consciously.

In reality, what we don't know can be a significant risk to our well-being. The fact that we choose to remain oblivious, ignorant or indifferent says all we need to know: that it is, in fact, something we must address. Intuition has no room for any form of incompetence.

Blinders are often harmful and stifling. Our refusal to face whatever we are avoiding robs us of an otherwise great opportunity to discover and acquire new experiences, perspectives and paths to mastery. All of which are essential elements for a strong intuition.

It is wise to identify our blinders so that we can examine where they come from, and begin to break them down.

History often serves as our principal reference point, and it tends to heavily influence our decisions. Because memory is so influential in experiences and decision-making, our personal history spawns blinders out of the best and the worst of times. Memories of the past can cause problems in the present and for the future.

For example, we may come out of a beautiful relationship that ends in our beloved's death. If so, the memory of that person can become an unhealthy standard we rigidly hold onto and use to evaluate whoever comes next. The problem is, measuring everyone else against the memory of a person who no longer exists and a relationship that is no longer possible places us in a closed or doubtful mindset in which new people and relationships will always fall short. Thus, the likelihood of finding love again is diminished. This mindset is manifested by impatience, unrealistic expectations, or the fact that we will never be ready to let go of what had been.

Women and men who come out of a traumatic and abusive relationship are also susceptible to blinders, fueled by fear, anxiety, and a lack of self-worth borne out of that negative experience. It makes it extremely hard to move forward due to an inability to trust others. To allow ourselves to love means we become vulnerable once again, and that can be scary. But we all want love and companionship in our lives, and we can achieve it. It requires time, a lot of it, to heal until we gain enough confidence. But if we don't, the blinders remain and strip us of the chance to happiness.

It would be unfair for both the next person and ourselves to enter a new relationship with blinders on. Not only that, the blinders may be preventing us from even considering a new relationship, resulting in unnecessary isolation.

I am familiar with how blinders can skew perception and hinder intuition in decision-making. For instance, my reliance on my uncle and disappointment with some people concerning my brother led me to create blinders when it came to how I could best be there for him. I felt powerless when my arrangement with my uncle fell through, and I started to lose faith in finding or creating a solution to send financial help for my brother. I was so close to giving up.

I'm usually objective, inquisitive, and persistent in finding solutions to problems. However, when it comes to my brother, who is very close to my heart, objectivity sometimes escapes me. My inability to help him had burdened me with guilt. I became more *reactive* than *proactive,* which clouded my judgement and formed a bias against everyone who was not my uncle. I didn't trust anyone else, even though I couldn't rely on him. It didn't help when my well-meaning uncle promised me that he'd be able to help again once he freed up some time. That kept me hoping, waiting, and wasting time. So with a lack of direction and clarity, I turned on my blinders and pushed my intuition out of the picture.

Finally, I decided to block out my thoughts and emotions for a little while, just to give it a rest. And once I rested my mind, the blinders just fell off and showed me what I needed to do!

Here's an example less personal to me, but surely familiar to you. The blinders that once emboldened countless cases of sexual harassment and assault in Hollywood are finally being removed. It is all over social media. Many celebrities who once seemed untouchable have fallen from their pedestals and been cast out. At the peak of the abuse, many of the victims found it difficult to get work if they stood up for themselves. They were alienated and cast out by influential personalities in the industry. The blinders that people wore took away their courage to stand up for what is right, and to right what is wrong. Hopefully, once the blinders are removed, things won't go back to the way they once were, and the industry will forever be changed for the better.

On an even grander scheme, anytime that human rights violations, exploitations, and repression flourish, it is primarily because people in positions of power and the people they have power over have their blinders on.

Blinders make us feel powerless. They hinder intuition by making us ineffective and limited in problem-solving.

The divisive and destructive consequences of having blinders on are evident all over the world. We see this manifested in:

— the many lives extinguished by extrajudicial killings,

— the idea that tyranny is better than a power vacuum, or that a power vacuum is better than tyranny,

— the belief that one religion or race is better than any other, resulting in genocide and other acts of terrorism,

— the idea that one skin colour is superior to any other, or

— the arrogant belief that humans are above all else (e.g. nature, animals, etc.).

For intuition to prevail and for us to experience its virtues — altruism, compassion, generosity, peace, harmony, and love — we start by removing our own blinders.

Peripheral Vision and Sidelights

Random House Dictionary defines *peripheral vision* as 'all that is visible to the eye outside the central area of focus', and *Cambridge Dictionary* defines *sidelight* as 'a piece of extra information that helps you understand something in a slightly new way'.

When we apply it to multidirectional thinking, it is that which we see outside of our centre. It may seem unimportant, inexplicit, or of little consequence, but once explored, it reveals the opposite. Peripheral vision allows us to see the sidelights that have an impact on our situation. Inasmuch as it is necessary for us to determine our centre, it is equally important to know what's happening just outside of it.

There will always be information in our periphery that — when given the opportunity to influence our thoughts — could provide answers that would cause us to shift course, benefiting our decision-making. We need to explore sidelights so that we know their related consequences.

For as long as we interact with people, there will always be influences coming at us, appearing in many forms, from different directions.

Sometimes, in order to arrive at our intended destination, it is wise to momentarily look away from what is readily in front of us and check the sidelights. We can liken it to wayfinding — when we evaluate alleyways or alternative paths that may seem unpopular or obscure but offer fresh perspective and possibility.

Our *peripheral vision* may lead us away from the major players in our life and introduce us to the minor players who are ready for promotion.

It is there to help us. How?

(1) Peripheral vision gives us a fuller appreciation of the information that is always there but ignored.

(2) It can identify new insightful patterns leading to different possibilities.

(3) When patterns and possibilities are adequately explored, it can yield beneficial outcomes.

We might think that these fortuitous details would always be subtle and difficult to discern since they are on the sidelight, but they're not. They only seem invisible because we don't bother to look, but become clear when we give them our attention. It might be challenging to spot the truly subtle ones immediately, but ignoring the sidelights that are plainly noticeable goes against what's natural.

The best way to look at our peripheral vision is to first remove our blinders and stop thinking about the issue in the same way. Furthermore, having a pause from thinking gives us a much-needed reprieve that does us a lot of good.

I have always worried about my brother living in the province on his own. I arrived at a point where I could not keep relying on some of my old channels to send help because they had either closed their doors or proved unscrupulous. I grew tired just thinking about it, so I stopped.

Once my mind had time to rest, and my blinders were gone, I tried looking at the sidelights. There, I was pleasantly surprised to find some people who had always been there to help but had remained pretty low-key.

Recently, I approached one lady to check if she had any news about my brother. I was delighted to find out that she owns a small eatery where my brother goes every day for his meals.

It was just perfect. I learned that her eatery is only a few doors away from where my brother stays. This wonderful lady has always been in the periphery helping my brother for quite some time now. But because she was low-key, I would never have known had I not explored further. She has now been 'promoted' to a significant player in our lives — for both my brother and me.

Through her, I can now even video chat with my brother and directly check on how he's doing. We've come to an arrangement where I prepay my brother's meals a month in advance to ensure he has freshly cooked and prepared breakfast, lunch and dinner every day. I no longer worry about his nourishment and well-being. She's been such a great help keeping me updated all the time! I'm grateful and hope for the best.

It's good practice to scour our periphery to explore other sources of answers. Again, awareness is key!

Imagine the strength of your intuition when you have achieved unconscious competence with these thinking methods!

Chapter 6   Intuition Tools

We've discussed some thinking methods that can help our brain to rewire and restructure itself and encourage the development of intuition. In this chapter, we're going to find tools to help us with our training. We need ones that will track our progress, further stimulate our mind and can be used daily.

Diary or Journal

For as long as I can remember, I have always appreciated the practice of recording my thoughts and experiences. I started keeping a diary in grade school. I found it therapeutic even before I knew what therapeutic meant. I spilt my thoughts and feelings onto its pages, especially those I couldn't share with others — such as the not-so-pleasant feelings I had for some people.

Throughout the years, my diary served as a form of self-talk that gave me hope when I was feeling down and opened my heart to freely express myself. It was a secret place where I could echo my thoughts, whatever they may be, without fear of retribution.

When I reread my diaries after some years, what I wrote made me uncomfortable. That was good because it meant I had gotten past that god-awful stage. It was great to witness how time and experience had shifted my perception of people and situations. It was also helpful to recognise the elements, especially those subtle yet pivotal ones, that influenced some of my decisions. My diaries were an extension of my memories and an excellent source of inspiration. They held the lessons that contributed to the maturation of my intuition.

I highly recommend you keep track of your thoughts and feelings by journaling too. It doesn't have to be difficult or time-consuming.

By sticking to the KISS practice of *keeping it short and straightforward*, a diary will effectively guide you to ask yourself the critical questions: the Whos, Whats, Wheres, Whens, Whys and Hows of your life. The answers would, at the very least, give you elements to reflect on that could lead to insight.

If you're also keeping track of health in your diary, it might be useful to take note of your nutritional intake and physical activity for the day too. Adding the products you use on your body (shampoos, soaps, lotions, oils, perfumes, etc.) might show you how they affect your health in the long run. Record the number of hours you slept, worked or were active. Your entries should be short and sweet, more like a quick journal highlighted in bullet points. That will help you make it a habit. Plus, it's easier to review brief notes than long tomes.

Some studies show that journaling — writing or recording our experiences and thoughts in a diary — has positive effects on our general health and well-being. Most especially when we are undergoing stressful events in our life. Eastern Michigan University student Briana Murnahan wrote in her honours thesis that a diary becomes a kind confidant and excellent source that helps:

(1) organise thoughts and feelings,

(2) reflect on changes,

(3) reduce stress and anxiety,

(4) monitor changes in self-esteem,

(5) address loneliness, and

(6) record milestones in our lives.

When we read other people's published diaries in the form of an autobiography, we find courage, relentlessness, persistence and awesomeness.

We have these qualities as well, but we'll never get to realise them unless we document our life and give ourselves the same chance to learn from and be inspired by it.

A diary can increase productivity and accountability and help us focus towards self-development. It makes us more mindful of our circumstances and the patterns we add to our repository of cues and triggers. It is critical to developing intuition.

Brainwave Frequencies and Entrainment

I struggled for weeks to finish this part of the book. I found it challenging to focus and process all the information I've collected about existing studies on brainwaves, the body's electrical processes and the current technologies that can improve our brain's performance. My inability to write and lack of productivity have frustrated me.

I wanted to include the method of *brainwave entrainment,* which I have found useful many times in the past.

What is *brainwave entrainment*? Brainworks Neuropathy defines it as 'a method to stimulate the brain into entering a specific state by using a pulsing sound, light, or electromagnetic field. The pulses elicit the brain's 'frequency following' response, encouraging the brainwaves to alight to the frequency of a given beat'. In other words, it's altering thought processes through sound.

So, to get through this writing impasse, I decided to listen to music which was configured to emit a beta frequency ranging between 12.5–30 Hz. Beta is the frequency that our brains enter when we are fully aware, processing information and making decisions. It is where we are fully engaged.

Rightly so, it helped me break my mental block — and allowed me to share my experience as an example of brainwave entrainment, without having to be paralysed from even more weeks of overthinking! I have always found it useful, yet I often use it as a last resort. It's in my nature to try to be disciplined about sorting out my own brain first, without any external influences. However, it is a wonderful tool when I need it.

Now, let's explore the different brainwaves and frequencies we emit, what they mean, and how we can use them to develop our intuition.

Brainwaves

Our brain, just like our heart, is a very hardworking organ. It never stops. It's always active even when we are asleep. And perhaps surprisingly, there is some limited brain activity even in a coma.

These activities are the electrical pulses generated by our neurons communicating with each other and detected as brainwaves by an electroencephalogram (EEG) or magnetoencephalogram (MEG).

There are five types of brainwaves that describe our levels of consciousness or awareness. They are alpha, beta, theta, delta and gamma waves. We measure them in cycles per second, also known as Hertz (Hz).

The different types of brainwaves indicate what our brain is doing. The lower the frequency, the less aware we are of our surroundings. We need all five types of brainwaves to stay healthy.

For consistency, all brainwave measurements in this book are based on the numbers from *Brainworks Neurotherapy*. However, be advised: There is some minor overlap in measurements across the scientific community, particularly with respect to identifying brainwaves as delta or theta between 3–4 Hz and beta or gamma between 30–38 Hz.

DELTA WAVES (.5–3 Hz)

Delta waves, also known as slow wave sleep, are prominent in very deep sleep. Sleepwalking and somniloquy (sleep talking) occur at this range. It can be challenging to wake a person up at this point of sleep. If we do, we will find them drowsy and confused. It is quite fascinating to note some measure the lowest frequency of delta waves at a mere 0.1 Hz. At 0 Hz, we reach complete inactivity — brain death.

A lack of delta waves during sleep can affect cognitive functions during waking hours. We feel sluggish, sleepy, low on energy, unable to focus, moody. We may manifest physical symptoms of a headache or experience other ill effects in our brain and thought processes.

Delta is a fundamental frequency our brains should regularly get into, with a good night's sleep, giving our bodies the time to rest and heal.

A prolonged lack of delta waves can have adverse effects on our health. After a while, we may exhibit brain fatigue, hallucinations, memory loss, or a weak immune system. Even death can occur if a lack of sleep lasts from 8–72 months, according to the study 'Slow Wave Sleep: Does It Matter?' by Thomas Roth, PhD.

THETA WAVES (3–8 Hz)

Theta waves are present during deep meditation, hypnotic or drowsy states, the first stage of sleeping, exploration, and spatial navigation. Low theta frequencies can be used to draw out childhood memories critical to addressing traumatic experiences during therapy sessions.

The theta state is also known as the twilight state. It dominates shamanic rituals and other hypnagogic practices in many cultures and can be induced in many ways from plant concoctions to rhythmic drum beats. These days, we can also enter into this trancelike state through brainwave entrainment using certain sounds or music.

ALPHA WAVES (8–12 Hz)

Alpha waves are also known as Berger's wave in honour of Hans Berger, the inventor of the EEG. They occur when we are awake, but in a relaxed state, particularly with our eyes closed.

Creativity or creative thinking lies within this range. It is the optimal brain state for visualisation and for mindful practices like reflection and meditation.

BETA WAVES (12–38 Hz)

Activities and functions such as reading, learning, performing tasks, concentrating, making decisions, and being fully engaged and aware generate beta waves. Beta waves represent our normal wakeful state.

While both alpha and beta waves are generally associated with being awake, it is interesting to learn that we also produce a combination of alpha and beta waves while experiencing rapid eye movement (REM), which is the time we typically dream in our sleep.

GAMMA WAVES (38–42 Hz, up to 150 Hz)

Gamma waves are also known as 'the seat of consciousness' for their presence during insight, memory, cognition, information processing, and attention. I believe gamma waves could also be the seat of intuition, which is a form of higher consciousness.

Long-term Buddhist meditation practitioners place themselves in this frequency during meditations focused on compassion.

It piqued my interest to learn that gamma waves develop in the young, peaking at around 4–5 years of age, right around the same time we start having imaginary friends. I connected the dots and realised that at this age children are still innocent and free from preconceived ideas that limit humans to believe only the kind of truth that can be seen or verified.

This childhood truth is pure intuition. Maybe the gamma waves that children tap into make it possible to see 'beyond the veil' and connect to what adults call (based on their perceived reality) imaginary, invisible, or fantasy.

Brainwave Entrainment

Now that we have an idea of the different brainwaves, their frequencies, and the states associated with each, we can look into how to use tools that allow us to elevate or synchronise our brainwave frequencies to a state that develops intuition. Brainwave entrainment is such a tool. How does it work?

Have you observed that it is the nature of things to get into synchrony? Have you seen live demonstrations or videos of several pendulums swinging according to their own timing or rhythm that — when placed together side-by-side — eventually end up synchronised? The same goes for metronomes, a murmuration of birds, a school of fish, and even women who end up having their periods around the same time after living together for a while.

Brainwave entrainment is the same principle. By exposing ourselves to a specific fixed wave frequency (beta, alpha, gamma, theta and delta), either by music, a flashing light or a combination of the two, our brainwaves will eventually be entrained or synchronised to such frequency.

Binaural beats, one type of brainwave entrainment, has been proven to influence memory, creativity, attention, anxiety, mood states and vigilance. It has also shown to either increase or decrease depression depending on the frequencies of the beats. A study called 'Auditory Beat Stimulation and its Effects on Cognition and Mood States', by Leila Chaieb, Elke Caroline Wilpert, Thomas P Reber, and Juergen Fell, showed that auditory beat stimulation, including binaural beats, may be a promising tool for the manipulation of cognitive processes and mood states.

Have you seen those old spy films that showed hypnosis or brainwashing using light and sound? I remember how they used to make me laugh because of the facial reactions and eyeball movements of the characters subjected to such activities. Now I realise there is a lot of truth to it, and it's no laughing matter.

Many studies prove combining light and sound can influence our brain functions, from putting us in a hypnotic state to getting into a trance.

This form of brainwave entrainment has useful applications for treating substance abuse, and in patients with ADHD. It is possible through biofeedback and photic stimulation, both covered extensively in scholarly articles by biofeedback pioneer Dr Thomas Budzynski.

Because of how it affects our brains, people with certain medical conditions such as photosensitivity, epilepsy and other brain disorders are advised to AVOID brainwave

Nature

We often hear people say that nature is the best medicine for the nerves and stress. A walk on the beach or in the woods, climbing a hill or even a mountain — the smell of flowers, of the earth — these activities and sensory experiences can give us a much-needed respite from the tensions of everyday life. With the demands of juggling so many roles every day — work, family, friends and self-care, it is no wonder many of us have forgotten to connect and recognise the things that genuinely matter. It seems to me that it has become more prevalent than ever to exclude self-care as part of our many responsibilities. This is a huge mistake and the root of almost all ailment.

The tasks that go along with our many obligations can either be beneficial or detrimental to us. They can be beneficial when used as an opportunity to deepen and nurture our intuition through mindful practice. But detrimental if laden with constant stressors and distractions that take away our ability to listen and connect — thereby drowning our intuition into total silence or even 'death'.

Nature is our solace, our haven. It is the saviour of intuition. I'm not just saying this because I feel and resonate with this personal truth, but because there is a particular vibration nature emits that is quite healing and completing. Some call it the Schumann resonances, or 'the healing heartbeats of mother earth'. I would call it a resonance void of the noisy and potentially harmful electromagnetic frequencies we cannot see. All of the electronic gadgets deemed necessary to keep up with the demands of the times emit them.

Communing with nature gives us the opportunity to unplug from all the harmful frequencies. It is not surprising to see how some people have taken to living off the grid, and found harmony in their lives by doing so.

However, *we do not need to go off the grid to unplug*. The technological noise we are trying to run away from, ironically, can offer some form of respite. And if we look and listen carefully, we can tap into the sights and sounds of nature as close as just outside the door.

When I don't have the chance to visit my favourite spot by the beach, I get relief from listening to the song of the birds in the morning and of the 'ruru' (morepork owl) at night in our backyard. I'm blessed to be living in a place where nature is practically everywhere around me!

When I am in the office and need to de-stress, I listen to recordings of the sounds of the ocean, the forest, and other natural scenarios courtesy of online videos or smartphone applications.

Of course, nothing can beat those times my husband and I drive to one of our favourite places, the giant windmills of Wellington. Driving can also connect us to nature. We see the trees along the way, the many lifestyle blocks (hobby farms, for you non-New Zealand folk) with their sheep, cows, and horses, and breathe in the earthy smell of the breeze.

Nature has a way of stimulating our senses and healing our mind, body, and spirit, if only we immerse ourselves in it. When our health is in excellent form, our senses fire on all cylinders, giving us a sharper, more heightened perception. This is an appreciable first step to intuiting.

Meditation

There are many meditation types and techniques available. All of them focus on awareness — whether it be our breath, our thoughts, our emotions, the sensation in our bodies, an object, the sounds around us, or whatever else we decide to pay attention to, meditation will cultivate a profound oneness within this *awareness without judgement.*

Such awareness conditions us to identify and filter the noise in our thoughts and emotions, which can result in clarity, sharper cognition and better decision making.

Some of the meditation types are Buddhist, Tibetan, Zen, transcendental, guided, and mindfulness meditations. They are all beneficial to our cognition and overall well-being, most especially in alleviating stress and pain. Meditation is not just meant to address stress and pain management. Used long-term, it can physically and physiologically alter our brain in the best way possible.

Studies have shown that long-term meditators have more grey matter, which is the part of the brain involved in muscle control, sensory perceptions, memory, speech, decision making, and self-control.

Meditation may offset grey matter atrophy as people age. Sara Lazar, a neuroscientist at Harvard Medical School, found a significant difference in the size of grey matter comparing 50-year-olds who meditated to those who did not. She was one of the first to show that anecdotal evidence of improved brain function in the minds of meditators could be supported scientifically in brain scans. In her scans, she found that long-term meditators had the same amount of grey matter in their prefrontal cortex as of 25-year-olds.

So she teamed up with Britta K. Hölzel of Technische Universität München to run another study, examining whether eight weeks of meditation could alter the brain. They found that it could. Besides increasing the grey matter, meditation increased the size of the hippocampus, responsible for cognition, memory, and emotional regulation. It increased the part of the brain associated with empathy and compassion. And it decreased the size of the amygdala, which is the part of the brain responsible for our fight, flight, freeze response in dealing with anxiety, fear, and stress.

Our fear, anxiety, and stress are intuition blockers. They keep the mind occupied in a detrimental way that spills over into our emotions and physical health, affecting our overall well–being. Our ability to manage, minimise or remove intuition blockers proportionately affects our ability to create the space we need for intuition to flourish.

Don't be afraid to try different meditation techniques until you find the one that works for you. A great teacher and a support group are helpful keys to a breakthrough. There are also many good meditation apps on your smartphone that can track your progress, as well as guided meditations available online.

Dreams

Everyone dreams, even if some of us can't remember. It takes practice and technique to recall them.

I had a student once who said she always forgot her dreams, but after she completed my 'Discover the Inner Workings of our World' class on *Dreams*, she was able to recall them and start a dream journal.

Dreaming is an essential process for our brain to sort, filter and file the memories of our experiences for the day. It is similar to purging and retaining the piles in your mind.

However, there is so much more to dreams than this as evidenced in the different cultures. Some believe that when we dream, we tread the thin line between our world and the 'otherworld(s)'. For some, dreams serve a purpose, primarily to guide us in our lives, most especially through tough times.

Dreams are personal and even intimate. We dream about what we think, see, do, fear and hope for. We dream of many themes, personalities and experiences including some strange ones.

We have been fascinated with dreams forever.

In the Bible, Joseph, the son of Jacob, became an influential figure in Egypt because of his ability to interpret dreams, saving Egypt from years of famine.

In science, Neil Bohr, considered the father of Quantum Mechanics, saw the mysterious structure of the atom appear like our solar system in his dream, with the sun at its centre.

Albert Einstein's dream of sliding down a mountainside at breakneck speed — the stars and the sky seeming to change as he approached the speed of light — inspired his theory of relativity.

There are many stories arising out of different cultures and spiritual practices of prophetic, groundbreaking and lifesaving dreams.

Let's explore to better understand what our dreams mean and how we can use them to strengthen our intuition.

From the previous chapter, we know that one of the practicalities of intuition is sleep, which is crucial to processing memories. Dreams are the manifestations of this process.

We now know that our memories are processed pretty much nonstop throughout the sleep cycle. It was previously thought that we dreamt only in REM sleep, but that has now been scientifically proven incorrect by multiple researchers. We actually dream during both REM and NREM sleep cycles, even if we don't remember most of our dreams.

REM and NREM sleep differ in the way they process our memories and in the kind of dreams they generate.

REM DREAMS

Most dreams that people remember occur during REM sleep. Hence they are called REM dreams. In REM dreams, we get to practice old experiences by freely associating old memories with new ones, or even imaginary circumstances.

REM dreams often appear vivid, wild, fantastical, far-out, and all sorts of other adjectives that can be used to defy logic. They are more uninhibited and incredible than their counterparts, and upon reflection — very intuitive. This free association that occurs in REM sleep is the key to creativity.

What's fantastic about REM dreams is that they serve as a safe space for us to experiment and try out whatever we can imagine without limitation or concern for consequences. REM sleep protects us from physical harm through natural muscle paralysis that occurs while in this sleep phase. That gives us the confidence to practice or test new ideas — sort of like being in an idea boot camp. Much of this is done unconsciously. But, we can also do this consciously through lucid dreaming, also known as conscious dreaming. We'll come back to that shortly.

NREM DREAMS

NREM dreams occur during the NREM sleep cycle. They are more realistic and familiar than their REM counterparts, and seemingly mundane. We don't generally remember them.

In NREM dreams, we often see the familiar faces of family members and friends. We dream of real-life situations in real places, and of normal activities such as walking, running, and driving a car, generally exhibited. NREM sleep can be compressed in short bursts.

Most people with sleep disorders such as sleepwalking, sleep terrors, and sleep-eating act during NREM sleep, when their protective muscle paralysis vanishes. Hence NREM dreams, regardless of how mundane they may appear, can move bodies into activities that overlap with the waking world, albeit with the absence of waking consciousness. As powerful as NREM dreams can be, focusing on the mundane makes them easy to forget.

In both REM and NREM sleep, our dreams reflect our waking world. They are both the abstract and the construct of all the elements that make us who we are — our thoughts, emotions, experiences, memories, and how we relate to our environment.

When we talk about using dreams as a tool to develop intuition, it's not just finding meaning in them. It's also about giving ourselves the freedom to do whatever we want within the safety of a dream state — without restrictions, a risk of harm, or real-world accountability. We are only limited by what we cannot imagine.

The best way to tap this valuable tool is to learn and practice lucid dreaming.

Lucid Dreaming

What is *lucid dreaming*? Also known as *hypnagogia,* it is essentially a sleep state that lies between sleep and wakefulness where we are aware that we are dreaming.

The goal of lucid dreaming is to direct movements, create intentions and purpose, and even go on a quest to find answers, make discoveries and form ideas as active aspects of our dreams.

One example is when I dream of flying, as many of us have likely experienced. What distinguishes an ordinary dream from a lucid dream is the *level of awareness or knowing*. I know that I am dreaming and therefore I am able to consciously control where and how I fly. I control the imaginary body movements I need to take the leap, stay afloat, glide through and fly against the wind, scout the environment, get to my destination, or merely enjoy it and be one with the sky!

In my dreams, I have flown through strange cities, familiar places, vast expanses and long mountain ranges. In one remarkable lucid dream, I flew along the stretch of an enchanted river by a beautiful castle where I shared great conversations with my great-grandfather Lolo Mama, the father of Lola Mommy. The fact that I was with Lolo Mama who had passed away many years before, and that I had flown to the imaginary castle where he lived was fantastically absurd and validated my awareness that I was dreaming.

I feel lighter, happier, and more empowered after every lucid dream I have.

My conversations with loved ones who have passed on, and the chance to reconnect with them, always gives me a sense of peace and reassurance. Most of all, the wisdom I gain in such cherished connections has proven invaluable, especially in my vocation of helping people find their path and answers. So when my clients say I am wise, I accept it with gratitude and humility because I attribute it as borrowed, or perhaps inherited, wisdom from my ancestors.

My lucid dreams have warned and guided me in times of critical transformation in my life that included discovering deceit, encouraging me not to give up, to be brave in pursuing a goal and showing me alternatives to solve my problems. Lucid dreaming has become a manifestation of my intuition that has guided and saved me many times.

There is an enormous source of references online and offline that could teach us how to lucid dream. However, be forewarned: without true desire and commitment, they are useless.

Dream Interpretation

Regardless of what or how we dream, we can find our dreams to be rich in archetypes, symbolism and hints (both bold and subtle), of what's going on in our lives. For this reason, I find dream interpretation another helpful tool for self-reflection that nurtures my intuition. Intuition speaks to us privately and directly through the symbolism in our dreams.

When we desire or need to interpret our dreams, we can do this through two different archetypes:

(1) collective archetypes, and

(2) personal archetypes.

Society formed *collective archetypes* throughout the ages. Meanings can significantly vary depending on culture, traditions and beliefs. They can be a good starting point for dream interpretation but have some limitations.

It's not unusual for some people I know to share their dreams with me and base their interpretation on an online or printed book dream dictionary. If this is the only way we interpret a dream, then I find it limiting. Yes, these archetypes have been formed by shared experiences, but some of them may not necessarily apply to us, or they could have become obsolete through changing times, or prove insufficient for many other reasons.

We form our *personal archetypes* based on our own experiences. They are unique, more meaningful, and speak to us about our past as well as our current circumstances and aspirations. They can be liberating and empowering since meanings evolve as we grow and mature.

Let's take the example of a dream about a mother. The collective meaning of mother as a dream archetype might be someone who is nurturing, loving, and healing. But that would not apply to someone who suffered emotional and mental abuse from their mother. In such an instance, the personal archetype of a mother becomes that of abuser or tormentor. And if the circumstances were brought about by substance abuse, then mother, as a personal archetype, could signify addiction, helplessness, or aspects leaning towards negativity.

Another example of a potential misinterpretation by using a collective archetype could be water. One collective interpretation of water is life. But to a person who has lost a loved one to drowning, the personal archetype of water could mean death or loss.

The personalities, objects, colours, places, and situations in our dreams require self-reflection to find our personal meaning. By remembering them, for as long as they are applicable, we add them to our repository of cues providing another avenue for intuition to communicate with and guide us.

If you want to further explore how to understand your dreams and learn to use them as a tool, you can do so in my other book, *Dreams: Discover the Inner Workings of our World, Book 2*, set to publish shortly after this book.

The Tarot

There are many misconceptions about the Tarot. It's been called:

— the devil's tool,

— all about the occult,

— scary,

— cursed,

— many other negative attributes bordering on the absurd and ridiculous.

These misconceptions are borne from superstitions and a lack of knowledge.

For starters, the Tarot is a deck of cards, made of paper, printed in colour or black-and-white, containing many images, numbers, titles, keywords, and scenarios that may depict everyday life or our fantastical imagination, depending on the Tarot deck of our choice.

Just like anything else, even the most beautiful thing can be the ugliest thing, depending on the mindset of the perceiver. I would recommend that people who are naturally cynical, pessimistic, and afraid skip exploring the Tarot as an intuition tool.

But for those who are open-minded, brave, and honest, the Tarot can be a pleasant surprise with respect to the manner in which it reflects our innermost thoughts and emotions. We need to be open to cultivating awareness to become proactive, wise, confident, and insightful, all of which hallmark a robust intuition.

The Tarot is similar to dreams in that it is rich in symbolism and archetypes that can be defined either collectively or personally.

It is another medium for self-reflection that has been my go-to tool for intuiting for many years now. Not just for myself, but most especially when guiding others.

The Deck

I have always admired the work of Salvador Dali. He is one of my favourite artists. When I found out that he created a complete Tarot deck for his beloved wife, I was so delighted. There was no way that I was not going to buy the Dali Tarot set, especially since it is his only artwork I would ever be able to afford.

There are many Tarot decks out there that are so beautiful, which is why I have turned into a collector. I consider each set an artistic masterpiece consisting of 78 cards, each beautifully and thoughtfully designed and painted by the artists. This variety makes it easy for anyone to choose a deck that genuinely resonates with them. That connection to your cards is fundamental when engaging with the Tarot.

Don't wait for someone to gift you with a special deck. If you find one you're drawn to, buy it.

There are two primary types of Tarot decks:

(1) those inspired by Rider-Waite-Smith, which are visually rich, and

(2) the Marseille type, which look more like ordinary playing cards, except that it includes the Major Arcana and extra court cards.

The Tarot has two parts:

(1) the Major Arcana with 22 cards starting with 0 (The Fool) to 21 (The World), and

(2) the Minor Arcana with 56 cards arranged into four suits (Swords, Cups, Wands, Pentacles). Each suit consists of:

(a) numbered cards from 1 to 10, and

(b) court cards, which are the Page, Knight, Queen, and King.

You can use the Major Arcana to look at the bigger picture or gain an overview, and the Minor Arcana to get into the details — the nitty-gritty.

Reflection

If you are an absolute novice with the Tarot, then congratulations! The keywords and societal archetypes associated with it have not yet conditioned you to a fixed and eventually limiting mindset towards their interpretation.

If you are familiar with the Tarot or have been using it for a while, then this simple method of reflection might come in handy whenever you feel stuck or stale regarding your connection with the cards. Hopefully, it will provide you with a fresher perspective.

The best possible way to start is to personally relate to one card at a time, following the steps outlined below.

1. Open your heart and mind.

2. Leave judgement behind.

3. Shuffle the deck.

4. Draw a card. One card is enough. Less is more. If you look at it and zoom into the details, you will have plenty of elements for reflection. Do not overwhelm yourself with more than one card.

5. Look into the card — as a whole and the images in it — like a mirror.

6. Use the images (people, animals, objects, backgrounds, colours, numbers) to reflect on:
— how you feel,
— the way you see yourself,
— the way you see others,
— the way you see the world,
— your hopes and fears,
— the things you expect,
— the things you are unsure of, and
— whatever you want to address.

7. Whatever comes to the surface needs digging. See how it stacks up and influences you concerning where you are by using the thinking methods, starting with the Triunity Approach. Always look at the positive and negative aspects, from which you can create your workable area (or middle ground).

8. Apply what you have created as your workable area in your decision-making.

9. Use it to propel and guide your plans.

10. Remember how your reflections can translate into actions and consequences.

You can also apply this method to Oracle or Angel cards, or any other form of visual representation, such as your favourite painting, a picture in a magazine, or whatever else you see that speaks to you.

If you want to further explore ways to understand and learn to use the Tarot as a tool, you can do so in my book *Tarot: Discover the Inner Workings of our World, Book 3*, set to publish shortly after *Dreams: Discover the Inner Workings of our World, Book 2.*

Part 5: Fantastical Intuition

Chapter 7   Back to The Beginning

Understanding intuition both scientifically and practically gives us the important elements we need to identify and assess our natural intuitive abilities, evaluate our strengths, and hone in on areas that need development. A practical understanding allows us to recognise that intuition is neither a fluke nor an airy-fairy concept. Rather it is a useful process that we can develop, apply, and hopefully master.

I wrote this book primarily to find the best possible answers to my questions about the nature of intuition, through ample research. I am satisfied with what I learned and what I have presented to you. However, there is also this part of intuition, which I call 'fantastical intuition', that I want to talk about. Because it exists. And no matter how crazy or kooky or illogical it may seem, we cannot sweep it under the rug. We need to talk about it.

Going back to the story about my brother at the beginning of the book, I can only try to analyse and do my best to make sense of how it happened.

In applying all the elements of intuition from ZIQ1 (perception, instinct, insight, intuition) and ZIQ2 (inheritance, environment, experience, memory), I could infer that there may be distinct patterns that I perceived, which made me receptive to such a vision or 'dream', for lack of a better word.

The patterns could include:

(1) a period of no communication with my brother,

(2) followed by the anxiety and worry brought about by my knowledge of his tendencies in how he interactions with others,

(3) and the fact that when these sorts of things had happened before, the people I usually would have heard from tended to see him less or not at all.

These could be the best logical explanation for my 'knowing without knowing how I knew' that something was wrong.

What remains inexplicable is my vision of him being attacked.

Was it a coincidence? I can't believe that it was. The only explanation I can turn to is to keep an open mind about the things that we know exist, but cannot explain — at least for the moment. *My inability to define the inner workings of fantastical intuition does not render it invalid.* And no expert can invalidate my visions of my brother. Not only do I know what I saw and what I felt that night, but I have experienced such intuition and visions about my brother a few times throughout the years. What are the probabilities of this happening more than once?

I believe that some of you may have had similar experiences as well.

It makes me think further about how fantastical intuition works. Was it my intuition or my brother's that made this connection? Could it be that as siblings we have the same fantastical intuition that connects us to this form of *vision messaging*?

Any manner of communication requires two parties, or two pieces of equipment — a transmitter and a receiver, which would make my brother the transmitter and me the receiver. It makes sense and may explain how I can connect with my clients during our Tarot readings.

In fact, a very interesting thing happened with me and my first-time client some time ago. I certainly thought I heard him mention a trip to a certain place in the US for his dream job while I was looking at and shuffling the Tarot cards for him. So I asked him when he is going (mentioning his dream job and the name of the place). He was shocked and asked me how I knew. I told him that he told me. And he said empathically, 'No ma'am, I did not tell you. I am 100% sure about this. It must be your intution.'

Ummm.. it's spooky even for me!

They transmit, I receive. I'm certain that there are others who can do both — transmit and receive.

Thoughts are energies which are electrical signals without mass — if only because we don't yet have the instrument to measure them.

Intuition is a thought, so it doesn't have mass. Thus, if intuition is massless (just like a photon), the only way it can travel is by the speed of light, which means it covers great distances in a blink of an eye. In physics, the special theory of relativity states that all massless particles — such as the photon and the gluon —must always move at the speed of light.

In other words, the term 'the speed of thought' doesn't just mean the speed at which thought is formed, but also the distance the thought travels. I believe this is partly how fantastical intuition works.

Another puzzle for me is how I'm able to connect with my clients. Though it appears that I provide them with insight, based on the feedback I get, the process of achieving this — not fully knowing who they are as individuals, and sometimes separated by thousands of kilometres between us — *must* be intuition at work. If I try to dig deeper, perhaps there are also patterns I have learned to unconsciously see and feel because of my experience with the many people I have guided throughout the years.

Patterns could show a troubled relationship, a lack of self-belief, an unfulfilling career, and so on, but saying these patterns exist and that's all it is oversimplifies how intuition works, which clearly can also be fantastical at times.

Even if there are universal truths that come up when I guide my clients, how can I explain some of the things that I get to know about them that I have no way of knowing because they never told me? This particular kind of knowing bordering on the fantastical does not happen in every reading, which is actually comforting because it leaves me with the many other times I *can* understand how and why intuition works.

There was a time when a person very close to me was lying through their teeth. I knew it, yet my affection became my blinders. I stayed in denial for the longest time. Through it all, intuition spoke to me through recurring dreams with my Lola Mommy warning me that the person was hiding in a body bag. The body bag represented all the secrets and deceit, and the death of the relationship.

When intuition works this way, it is difficult, even for me, to measure, analyse, and make sense of. It is something that cannot be quantified. The best thing we can do for now is trust, hope, and believe that one day more and more will be understood.

Perhaps fantastical intuition is similar to quantum physics, where reason and logic cease as we reach farther from the macro world. The principles and processes of fantastical intuition would appear unreasonable and illogical compared with real-world intuition. So why limit 'quantum' to physics? Why not explore the possibilities of quantum intuition?

I call the inexplicable, magical, and unbelievable form of intuition 'fantastical intuition', for lack of a proper term. I thought of quantum intuition, but I did not want to bastardise the word quantum, even if its crazy aspects keep bringing me back to the idea that fantastical intuition is the 'quantum physics of intuition'.

We have barely scraped the surface of what real-world intuition is. Once we have built a solid understanding of it, then perhaps fantastical intuition will be next.

Or maybe it will work the other way around. By understanding and being open to fantastical intuition, real-world intuition will be more easily understood.

What do you think?

Appendix :
Sources arranged per chapter and in alphabetical order

Introduction

Part 1 : Overview

Chapter 1   Intuition?

What's in a word?

Intuition. (n.d.). Retrieved from
https://en.oxforddictionaries.com/definition/intuition

Intuition.(n.d.). Retrieved from
http://dictionary.cambridge.org/dictionary/english/intuition

Sadler-Smith, E. (2012, August 06). Inside Intuition. Retrieved from
https://books.google.co.nz/books?id=PiNbBAAAQBAJ&source=gbs_navlinks_s

Walker, T. (1995). Elemental Wisdom in Teacher Training. Retrieved from
.https://dalspacelibrary.dal.ca/bitstream/handle/10222/55073/NN05311.PDF?sequence=1

Intuition at work

Fischbein, H. (2002). Intuition in Science and Mathematics -
An educational Approach. Retrieved from
http://www.springer.com/gp/book/9789027725066

Frantz, R. (2006, July 02). Two Minds: Intuition and Analysis
in the History of Economic Thought. Retrieved from

https://books.google.co.nz/books?id=seBayzineiAC&printsec=f
rontcover#v=onepage&q&f=false

Google.com (2017, November 23). Search parameters:
Studies on Intuition. Retrieved from https://www.google.com

Harvey, I. (2013, October 09). Intuitive Traders. Retrieved
from https://www.investopedia.com/university/introduction-
stock-trader-types/intuitive-traders.asp

Raami, A. (2015). INTUITION UNLEASHED. Helsinki: Aalto
University. Retrieved from http://www.aalto.fi/en/midcom-
serveattachmentguid-
1e4c66697f50d52c66611e48992db3bcb01db3fdb3f/doctoral_di
ssertation_asta_raami.pdf

Woolley, A., BA, & Kostopoulou, O., MSc, PhD. (2013, January
24). Clinical Intuition in Family Medicine: More Than First
Impressions. Retrieved from
http://www.annfammed.org/content/11/1/60.full

Intuition Network

Garfield.library.upenn.edu (1980). Multiple Independent
Discovery & Creativity in Science. Essays of an Information
Scientist, 4(44), 1979-80, 660-665. Retrieved from
http://www.garfield.library.upenn.edu/essays/v4p660y1979-
80.pdf

Nobelprize.org (2015, October 6). The Nobel Prize in Physics 2015. Retrieved from https://www.nobelprize.org/nobel_prizes/physics/laureates/2015/press.html

Piepmeyer, A. (2007). Collective consciousness. Retrieved December 11, 2017, from http://csmt.uchicago.edu/glossary2004/collectiveconsciousness.htm

Part 2 : The Inner Workings of Intuition

Chapter 2   Intuiting

Adams, L. (2017). Learning a New Skill is Easier Said Than Done. Retrieved from http://www.gordontraining.com/free-workplace-articles/learning-a-new-skill-is-easier-said-than-done/

Coraci, F. (Director), Sandler, A., Giarraputo, J., Moritz, N. H., Koren, S. W., & OKeefe, M. (Producers), & Koren, S. W., & OKeefe, M. (Writers). (2006). Click [Motion picture]. United States: Sony Pictures Entertainment.

Enacademic.com. (2010). Four stages of competence. Retrieved December 11, 2017, from http://enacademic.com/dic.nsf/enwiki/679884

Enacademic.com. (2010). Johari window. Retrieved from http://enacademic.com/dic.nsf/enwiki/509517#cite_note-date-0

Frantz, R. (2006). Two Minds: Intuition and Analysis in the History of Economic Thought. Retrieved from https://books.google.co.nz

ZIQ1 - The Intuition Process

Perception

En.oxforddictionaries.com (2017). Perception. Retrieved from https://en.oxforddictionaries.com/definition/perception

Etymonline.com (2017). Perceive. Retrieved from https://www.etymonline.com/word/perceive

Sekuler, R. and Blake, R. (1994). Perception 3rd International Edition. McGraw Hill, Singapore.

Instinct

Dictionary.cambridge.org (2017). Instinct. Retrieved from https://dictionary.cambridge.org/dictionary/english/instinct

Etymonline.com (2017). Instinct. Retrieved from Retrieved from https://www.etymonline.com/word/instinct

Nicholson, N. (2014, July 31). How Hardwired Is Human Behavior? Retrieved from https://hbr.org/1998/07/how-hardwired-is-human-behavior

YouTube (2017). ABC News: 10 Heroic Kids Who Came to the Rescue | ABC News Remix. Retrieved from https://www.youtube.com/watch?v=5l0sR191G2Y

YouTube (2017). ViralHog: Superhero Dad Saves His Children with Lightning Fast Response. Retrieved from https://www.youtube.com/watch?v=C_qsSaEm4sA

Insight

En.oxforddictionaries.com (2017). Insight. Retrieved from
https://en.oxforddictionaries.com/definition/insight

Etymonline.com (2017). Insight. Retrieved from
https://www.etymonline.com/word/insight

Evans, T. (2011). The Art and Science of Light Bulb Moments.
Retrieved from
https://books.google.co.nz/books?id=8lN1oeEkjccC&printsec=f
rontcover#v=onepage&q&f=false

Medical-dictionary.thefreedictionary.com (2017). Insight.
Retrieved from
http://medical-dictionary.thefreedictionary.com/insight

Sternberg, Robert & E. Davidson, Janet. (1983). Insight in the
gifted. Educational Psychologist - EDUC PSYCHOL. 18. 51-57.
10.1080/00461528309529261.
Retrieved from
https://www.researchgate.net/publication/254303516_Insight
_in_the_gifted

TripAdvisor.com (2017). Tarot Zamm. Retrieved from
https://www.tripadvisor.co.nz/Attraction_Review-g255115-
d2449588-Reviews-Tarot_Zamm-
Wellington_Greater_Wellington_North_Island.html

Intuition

Bolte, A., Goschke, T., & Kuhl, J. (2003, September). Emotion
and intuition. Retrieved from
https://www.ncbi.nlm.nih.gov/pubmed/12930470

Roddenberry, G. (Producer). (1966). *Star Trek* [Video file]. United States: Desilu Productions, Norway Corporation, Paramount Television. Retrieved from http://www.imdb.com/title/tt0060028/?ref_=ttco_co_tt

Tarotreader.co.nz (2017). Testimonials - What Clients Say. (n.d.). Retrieved from http://www.tarotreader.co.nz/what-clients-say/

ZIQ2 - The Fundamental Factors of Intuition

Genetics

Angier, N. (1997, June 11). Parental Origin of Chromosome May Determine Social Graces, Scientists Say. Retrieved from http://www.nytimes.com/1997/06/12/us/parental-origin-of-chromosome-may-determine-social-graces-scientists-say.html

Epigenetics

Association for Psychological Science. (2016, June 6). Genetic variations linked with social, economic success. Retrieved from https://www.sciencedaily.com/releases/2016/06/160606142900.htm

Beard, A. (2017, August 04). Is Your Success Really Shaped by Your Genes? Retrieved from https://hbr.org/2017/01/your-success-is-shaped-by-your-genes

Biblehub.com. (2017). Numbers 14:18. Retrieved from http://biblehub.com/numbers/14-18.htm

Hamzelou, J. (2016, June 7). Genetic test predicts your success in life, but not happiness. Retrieved from https://www.newscientist.com/article/2092757-genetic-test-predicts-your-success-in-life-but-not-happiness/

Klosin, A., Casas, E., Hidalgo-Carcedo, C., Vavouri, T., &
Lehner, B. (2017, April 21). Transgenerational transmission of
environmental information in C. elegans. Retrieved from
http://science.sciencemag.org/content/356/6335/320

Veenendaal, M. V., Painter, R. C., De, S. R., Bossuyt, P. M.,
Van, J. A., Gluckman, P. D., Roseboom, T. J. (2013, April).
Transgenerational effects of prenatal exposure to the 1944-45
Dutch famine. Retrieved from
https://www.ncbi.nlm.nih.gov/pubmed/23346894

Whatisepigenetics.com. (2013, July 30). A Super Brief and
Basic Explanation of Epigenetics for Total Beginners. Retrieved
from https://www.whatisepigenetics.com/what-is-epigenetics/

Whatisepigenetics.com (2017). Epigenetics: Fundamentals,
History, and Examples. (n.d.). Retrieved from
https://www.whatisepigenetics.com/fundamentals/

Physiology

Bedard, A. J., Jr. (1999, January). Naturally occurring sources
of infrasound. Retrieved from
http://asa.scitation.org/doi/abs/10.1121/1.425166 The Journal
of the Acoustical Society of America 105, 1103 (1999);
https://doi.org/10.1121/1.425166

Cicero, S. (2009, August 20). The Sense of Touch. Retrieved
from http://health.howstuffworks.com/skin-
care/information/anatomy/touching.htm/printable

Draper, S. (2005, October 20). How many senses do humans
have? Retrieved December 10, 2017, from
http://www.psy.gla.ac.uk/~steve/best/senses.html

Endsley, K. (n.d.). What Is Seismology? Retrieved from
http://www.geo.mtu.edu/UPSeis/waves.html

Ouellette, J. (2015, October 30). Some 'Ghosts' May Be Sound Waves Just Below Human Hearing. Retrieved from https://www.gizmodo.com.au/2015/10/some-ghosts-may-be-sound-waves-just-below-human-hearing/

Pedia Press. (2017). Cats. Retrieved from https://books.google.co.nz/books?id=UYGn7z-7tmAC&printsec=frontcover#v=onepage&q&f=false

Raval, R. (2014, May 09). INFRASOUND – the frequency of fear. Retrieved from http://www.mushroom-magazine.com/infrasound-frequency-fear/

School of Medical Sciences. (2012). Physiology. Retrieved from https://medicalsciences.med.unsw.edu.au/students/disciplines/physiology

Syufy, F. (2017, October 03). Learn About Cats' Superior Sense of Smell. Retrieved from https://www.thespruce.com/sense-of-smell-552117

TheFreeDictionary.com (2017). Exteroception. (n.d.). Retrieved from http://www.thefreedictionary.com/exteroception

TheFreeDictionary.com (2017). Interoception. (n.d.). Retrieved from https://www.thefreedictionary.com/interoception

The Heroes of Mt. Everest

Editors. (2017, September 07). Mitochondrion: Definition, Structure and Function. Retrieved from https://biologydictionary.net/mitochondrion/

Gilbert-Kawai, E. T., Milledge, J. S., Grocott, M. P., & Martin, D. S. (2014, November 1). King of the Mountains: Tibetan and Sherpa Physiological Adaptations for Life at High Altitude. Retrieved from http://physiologyonline.physiology.org/content/29/6/388

Mosedale, T. (2017). Using Oxygen. Retrieved from http://everestexpedition.co.uk/everest/using-oxygen/

Senthilingam, M. (2016, October 07). The biological secrets that make Sherpas superhuman mountaineers. Retrieved from http://edition.cnn.com/2015/11/11/health/sherpas-superhuman-mountaineers/

Sohn, E. (2017, March 12). How Does A Nepalese Porter Carry So Much Weight? Retrieved from https://www.npr.org/sections/goatsandsoda/2017/03/12/5179 23490/how-does-a-nepalese-sherpa-carry-so-much-weight

Time Inc. (1999, June 06). TIME 100 Persons of The Century. Retrieved from http://content.time.com/time/magazine/article/0,9171,26473, 00.html

UMDF.org (2017, November 29). What is Mitochondrial Disease? Retrieved from

https://www.umdf.org/what-is-mitochondrial-disease/

Double D - Design and Discipline

Allen, R. (2011, December 11). Michael Phelps Workout and Diet. Retrieved from https://www.muscleprodigy.com/michael-phelps-workout-and-diet/

Koebler, J. (2016, August 08). The Science of Michael Phelps's Gold Medal-Winning Turn. Retrieved from https://motherboard.vice.com/en_us/article/wnxzyn/michael-phelps-gold-medal-dolphin-kick-turn

Siebert, V. (2014, April 25). Michael Phelps: The man who was built to be a swimmer. Retrieved from http://www.telegraph.co.uk/sport/olympics/swimming/10768083/Michael-Phelps-The-man-who-was-built-to-be-a-swimmer.html

Taylor, T. (2016, August 7). How Michael Phelps's body has changed since London. Retrieved from https://www.si.com/olympics/2016/08/07/michael-phelps-rio-olympics-recovery

Work Our Info Guru. (2017). Michael Phelps Workout Routine. Retrieved from https://workoutinfoguru.com/michael-phelps-workout/

The Colour of Music

Bor, D., Rothen, N., Schwartzman, D. J., Clayton, S., & Seth, A. K. (2014, November 18). Adults Can Be Trained to Acquire Synesthetic Experiences. Retrieved from https://www.nature.com/articles/srep07089

Chiou, R., Stelter, M., & Rich, A. N. (2012, April 27). Beyond colour perception: Auditory–visual synaesthesia induces experiences of geometric objects in specific locations. Retrieved from https://www.sciencedirect.com/science/article/pii/S0010945212001323

Grossenbacher, P. G., & Lovelace, C. T. (2001, January 26). Mechanisms of synesthesia: cognitive and physiological constraints. Retrieved from http://www.sciencedirect.com/science/article/pii/S1364661300015710

MedicineNet.com. (2016, September 6). Medical Definition of Chromesthesia. Retrieved from https://www.medicinenet.com/script/main/art.asp?articlekey=39049
Original source: http://www.daysyn.com/GrossenbacherLovelace2001.pdf

Environment

Personal Environment

Social Environment

Barnett, E., PhD, & Casper, M., PhD. (2011, October 10). A definition of "social environment". Retrieved from http://ajph.aphapublications.org/doi/abs/10.2105/AJPH.91.3.465a

Kirst-Ashman, K. (2007, February 27). Human Behavior, Communities, roups iOrganizations, and Gn the Macro Social Environment: An Empowerment Approach. Retrieved from https://books.google.co.nz/books?id=08pmXNH6frAC&printsec=frontcover#v=onepage&q&f=false

ScotPHO. (2017, January 24). Social environment: introduction. Retrieved from http://www.scotpho.org.uk/life-circumstances/social-environment/introduction

The Heart and the Hearth

Ohikuare, J. (2014, January 21). Life as a Nonviolent Psychopath. Retrieved from https://www.theatlantic.com/health/archive/2014/01/life-as-a-nonviolent-psychopath/282271/

Stromberg, J. (2013, November 22). The Neuroscientist Who Discovered He Was a Psychopath. Retrieved from https://www.smithsonianmag.com/science-nature/the-neuroscientist-who-discovered-he-was-a-psychopath-180947814/

Washington, G. (2015, July 10). The Scientist and the Psychopath. Retrieved from https://www.npr.org/2015/07/10/421625310/the-scientist-and-the-psychopath

Culture

Jeong-Ook, L., Myung-jin, K., Irwin, M., Nesbitt, R. E., & Peng, K. (2009). East and West. Retrieved from http://www.worldcat.org/title/east-and-west/oclc/463466324

Publisher: Wheeling, IL : Film Ideas. Presented by Korea Educational Broadcast System. Watch the film https://www.youtube.com/watch?v=ZoDtoB9Abck and https://www.youtube.com/watch?v=709jjq8qk0k.

Open.lib.umn.edu (2016, April 08). Sociology: Understanding and Changing the Social World. Retrieved from http://open.lib.umn.edu/sociology/chapter/3-2-the-elements-of-culture/

The Gist of the Matter

Voices

Luhrmann, T. M., Padmavati, R., Tharoor, H., & Osei, A. (2014). Differences in voice-hearing experiences of people with psychosis in the USA, India and Ghana: interview-based study. The British Journal of Psychiatry, 206(1), 41-44. doi:10.1192/bjp.bp.113.139048

Experiences and Development

Memory, Learning and Identity

Horgan, J. (2014, July 14). Scientific Heretic Rupert Sheldrake on Morphic Fields, Psychic Dogs and Other Mysteries. Retrieved from https://blogs.scientificamerican.com/cross-check/scientific-heretic-rupert-sheldrake-on-morphic-fields-psychic-dogs-and-other-mysteries/

Human-memory.net (2017). WHAT IS MEMORY? Retrieved from http://www.human-memory.net/intro_what.html

MacDonald, F. (2016, October 26). An English-Speaking Teenager Has Woken Up From a Coma Speaking Fluent Spanish. Retrieved from https://www.sciencealert.com/people-keep-waking-up-from-head-injuries-speaking-a-different-language

MacIsaac, T. (2014, May 17). 3-Year-Old Remembers Past Life, Identifies Murderer and Location of Body. Retrieved from https://www.theepochtimes.com/uplift/3-year-old-remembers-past-life-identifies-murderer-and-location-of-body_681034.html

Neal, M. (2012, June 08). Suffers head injury, becomes musical prodigy . Retrieved from http://www.nydailynews.com/news/national/acquired-savant-derek-amato-musical-prodigy-hitting-head-hard-diving-shallow-pool-article-1.1091812

Noble, F. (2016, February 12). Man who woke from a coma speaking fluent MANDARIN after a car accident goes on a Chinese dating show - and finds a girlfriend. Retrieved from http://www.dailymail.co.uk/news/article-3443540/Man-woke-coma-speaking-fluent-MANDARIN-car-accident-goes-Chinese-dating-finds-girlfriend.html

Payton, M. (2016, June 02). Italian man suffers brain damage and now eats, reads and speaks French. Retrieved from http://www.independent.co.uk/news/world/europe/italian-man-suffers-brain-damage-and-now-speaks-french-and-france-compulsive-foreign-language-a7061001.html

Raatikainen, P. (2013, November 11). Gödel's Incompleteness Theorems. Retrieved from https://plato.stanford.edu/entries/goedel-incompleteness/#PhiImpAll

The Telegraph. (2010, April 12). Croatian teenager wakes from coma speaking fluent German. Retrieved from http://www.telegraph.co.uk/news/worldnews/europe/croatia/7583971/Croatian-teenager-wakes-from-coma-speaking-fluent-German.html

Warren , L. (2015, February 19). Furniture store worker who was mugged and woke up a math genius tells how his life was turned upside down. Retrieved from http://www.dailymail.co.uk/news/article-2959038/Woman-chaser-woke-math-genius-knocked-muggers-says-not-change-brutal-attack.html

Part 3 : The Practicalities of Intuition

Chapter 4   The dependencies of intuition

Know thyself

Health and lifestyle

Diet and essential nutrients

Choi, S., & Friso, S. (2010, November 01). Sang-Woon Choi. Retrieved from http://advances.nutrition.org/content/1/1/8.full

Brain

Delarue, J., Matzinger, O., Binnert, C., Schneiter, P., Chioléro, R., & Tappy, L. (2003, June). Fish oil prevents the adrenal activation elicited by mental stress in healthy men. Retrieved from https://www.ncbi.nlm.nih.gov/pubmed/12909818

Gómez-Pinilla, F. (2008, July). Brain foods: the effects of nutrients on brain function. Retrieved from https://www.ncbi.nlm.nih.gov/pmc/articles/PMC2805706/

Nature Reviews. Neuroscience, 9(7), 568–578. http://doi.org/10.1038/nrn2421

UHN Staff. (2017, November 9). How to Recognize High Cortisol Symptoms. Retrieved from https://universityhealthnews.com/daily/depression/how-to-recognize-high-cortisol-symptoms/

Yates, D. (2017, May 18). Healthy brain aging linked to omega-3 and omega-6 fatty acids in the blood. Retrieved from https://www.sciencedaily.com/releases/2017/05/170518140235.htm

Eyes

Adler, R., MD. (2016, December). Dry Eye Syndrome Causes and Symptoms. Retrieved from http://www.allaboutvision.com/conditions/dryeye-syndrome.htm

Heiting, G., OD. (2017, March). Eye Benefits of Omega-3 Fatty Acids. Retrieved from http://www.allaboutvision.com/nutrition/fatty_acid_1.htm

Heiting, G., OD. (2016, August). Vitamin C and Bioflavonoids: Powerful Eye Antioxidants. Retrieved from http://www.allaboutvision.com/nutrition/vitamin_c.htm

Kozarsky, A., MD. (2017, March 24). Understanding Vision Problems -- Prevention. Retrieved from http://www.webmd.com/healthy-aging/guide/understanding-vision-problems-prevention

National Eye Institute. (2015, September 01). Facts About Age-Related Macular Degeneration. Retrieved from https://nei.nih.gov/health/maculardegen/armd_facts

NZ Nutrition Foundation. (2013, April). Vitamin E. Retrieved from https://www.nutritionfoundation.org.nz/nutrition-facts/vitamins/vitamin-e

Shalev, I., Moffitt, T. E., Wong, T. Y., Meier, M. H., Houts, R. M., Ding, J., . . . Poulton, R. (2013, July 01). Retinal Vessel Caliber and Lifelong Neuropsychological Functioning: An Investigative Tool for Cognitive Epidemiology. Retrieved from https://www.ncbi.nlm.nih.gov/pmc/articles/PMC3713191/

SpecsaversOfficial. (2011, October 15). Specsavers 'Sauna' advert. Retrieved from https://www.youtube.com/watch?v=VELQ39QAYP4

University of Maryland Medical Center. (2015, March 23). Beta-carotene. Retrieved from http://www.umm.edu/health/medical/altmed/supplement/beta carotene

University of Maryland Medical Center. (2015, August 5). Omega-3 fatty acids. Retrieved from http://www.umm.edu/health/medical/altmed/supplement/omega3-fatty-acids

University of Maryland Medical Center. (2015, August 5). Vitamin A (Retinol). Retrieved from http://www.umm.edu/health/medical/altmed/supplement/vitamin-a-retinol

University of Maryland Medical Center. (2013, July 13). Zinc. Retrieved from http://www.umm.edu/health/medical/altmed/supplement/zinc

WebMD. (n.d.). Vitamins: Their Functions and Sources - Topic Overview. Retrieved from https://www.webmd.com/vitamins-and-supplements/tc/vitamins-their-functions-and-sources-topic-overview#1

White, T. (2007, April 11). Eye diseases changed great painters' vision of their work later in their lives. Retrieved from https://news.stanford.edu/news/2007/april11/med-optart-041107.html

Ears

Choi, Y., Miller, J. M., Tucker, K. L., & Hu, A. H. (2014, January 01). Antioxidant vitamins and magnesium and the risk of hearing loss in the US general population. Retrieved from http://ajcn.nutrition.org/content/99/1/148.full

Resnick, S., PhD, Kraut, M. A., MD, PhD, Ferrucci, L., MD, & An, Y., MS. (2014, January 22). Hearing Loss Linked to Accelerated Brain Tissue Loss - 01/22/2014. Retrieved from https://www.hopkinsmedicine.org/news/media/releases/hearing_loss_linked_to_accelerated_brain_tissue_loss

Vestibular Disorders Association (VEDA). (2015, December 28). Dietary Considerations. Retrieved from http://vestibular.org/understanding-vestibular-disorders/treatment/vestibular-diet

Smell and Taste

Fried, M. P., MD. (n.d.). Overview of Smell and Taste Disorders - Ear, Nose, and Throat Disorders. Retrieved from http://www.merckmanuals.com/home/ear,-nose,-and-throat-disorders/symptoms-of-nose-and-throat-disorders/overview-of-smell-and-taste-disorders

Spence, C. (2015, November 02). Just how much of what we taste derives from the sense of smell? Retrieved from https://flavourjournal.biomedcentral.com/articles/10.1186/s13411-015-0040-2

The Nose that Knows

Bromley, S. M., MD. (2000, January 15). Smell and Taste Disorders: A Primary Care Approach. Retrieved December 13, 2017, from https://www.aafp.org/afp/2000/0115/p427.html

Hummel, T., Heilmann, S., & Hüttenbriuk, K. B. (2002, November). Lipoic acid in the treatment of smell dysfunction following viral infection of the upper respiratory tract. Retrieved from https://www.ncbi.nlm.nih.gov/pubmed/12439184

Invisibilia. (2015, January 15). Disappearing Fear. Retrieved from https://www.npr.org/2015/01/16/377519199/disappearing-fear

Kruse, R. A., & Cambron, J. A. (2011, December). A possible correlation between vitamin D deficiency and loss of smell: 2 case reports. Retrieved from https://www.ncbi.nlm.nih.gov/pmc/articles/PMC3315864/

Smart Publications. (2010, October 27). Human Pheromones: The Science Behind the Scent of Attraction | Smart Publications. Retrieved from http://www.smart-publications.com/articles/human-pheromones-the-science-behind-the-scent-of-attraction

Buddy Buds

Bradbury, J. (2004, March 16). Taste Perception: Cracking the Code. Retrieved from http://journals.plos.org/plosbiology/article?id=10.1371%2Fjournal.pbio.0020064 doi: https://doi.org/10.1371/journal.pbio.0020064

Bramen, L. (2010, May 07). Mamas, Don't Let Your Babies Grow Up to Be Broccoli-Haters. Retrieved from https://www.smithsonianmag.com/arts-culture/mamas-dont-let-your-babies-grow-up-to-be-broccoli-haters-87592394/

Breslin, P. A. (may 6, 2013). An Evolutionary Perspective on Food Review and Human Taste. Current Biology , 23(9), R409-R418 doi: http://dx.doi.org/10.1016/j.cub.2013.04.010

Bromley, S. M., MD. (2000, January 15). Smell and Taste Disorders: A Primary Care Approach. Retrieved December 13, 2017, from https://www.aafp.org/afp/2000/0115/p427.html

Hadhazy, A. (2011, December 30). Tip of the Tongue: Humans May Taste at Least 6 Flavors. Retrieved from https://www.livescience.com/17684-sixth-basic-taste.html

Kerchner, M. S. (2013, July 12). A Sense of Taste: Nurture or Nature? Retrieved from http://fitnessandwellnessnews.com/a-sense-of-taste-nurture-or-nature/

Quinn, B. (2009, February 15). Vitamin deficiencies can alter your taste buds. Retrieved from http://articles.chicagotribune.com/2009-02-15/features/0902110331_1_taste-sensations-taste-buds-folic-acid

Skin and Touch

Oxford University Press. (2001). Visceral sensation. Retrieved from http://www.encyclopedia.com/medicine/encyclopedias-almanacs-transcripts-and-maps/visceral-sensation

Touch of Hope

Chandler, S. (2017, October 03). Can Calcium Be Absorbed Without Magnesium? Retrieved from https://www.livestrong.com/article/444390-can-calcium-be-absorbed-without-magnesium/

Schagen, S. K., Zampeli, V. A., Makrantonaki, E., & Zouboulis, C. C. (2012, July 01). Discovering the link between nutrition and skin aging. Retrieved from https://www.ncbi.nlm.nih.gov/pmc/articles/PMC3583891/

Wax, E., RD, Zieve, D., MD, MHA, Conaway, B., & A.D.A.M. Editorial team. (2017, January 7). Vitamin C. Retrieved from https://medlineplus.gov/ency/article/002404.htm

Muscle and joints

Axe, J., Dr. (2017, December 11). Top 10 Magnesium Rich Foods Plus Proven Benefits. Retrieved from https://draxe.com/magnesium-deficient-top-10-magnesium-rich-foods-must-eating/

Dai, Q., Motley, S. S., Jr., J. A., Concepcion, R., Barocas, D., Byerly, S., & Fowke, J. H. (2011, April 25). Blood Magnesium, and the Interaction with Calcium, on the Risk of High-Grade Prostate Cancer. Retrieved from http://journals.plos.org/plosone/article?id=10.1371%2Fjournal.pone.0018237
https://doi.org/10.1371/journal.pone.0018237

Derrer, D. T., MD. (2016, March 20). Top Foods for Calcium and Vitamin D. Retrieved from https://www.webmd.com/food-recipes/guide/calcium-vitamin-d-foods

Blood vessels

American Pregnancy Association. (2015, July). Folic Acid: What Foods Have it? Retrieved from http://americanpregnancy.org/pregnancy-health/folic-acid/

Axe, J., Dr. (2017, August 09). Top 10 Potassium-Rich Foods & Potassium Benefits. Retrieved from https://draxe.com/top-10-potassium-rich-foods/

Cleveland Clinic. (n.d.). Heart & Blood Vessels: Blood Flow. Retrieved from https://my.clevelandclinic.org/health/articles/17059-heart--blood-vessels-how-does-blood-travel-through-your-body

Daily Mail Australia. (2001, July 18). Circulatory system: Blood vessels. Retrieved from http://www.dailymail.co.uk/health/article-10976/Circulatory-Blood-vessels.html

Dieticians of Canada. (2017, March 7). Food Sources of Vitamin B12. Retrieved from https://www.dietitians.ca/Your-Health/Nutrition-A-Z/Vitamins/Food-Sources-of-Vitamin-B12.aspx

IMedix. (n.d.). Blood circulation effects on energy level. Retrieved from https://medical-dictionary.thefreedictionary.com/Blood%20circulation%20effects%20on%20energy%20level

Singh, S., & Mishra, S. (2013, May & June). Aging and Nutrition: A Review Article. Retrieved from http://www.iosrjournals.org/iosr-jnhs/papers/vol1-issue4/H0144347.pdf?id=1613

The Franklin Institute. (2017, May 19). Blood Vessels. Retrieved from https://www.fi.edu/heart/blood-vessels

The Nutrition Source. (2015, May 26). Omega-3 Fatty Acids: An Essential Contribution. Retrieved from https://www.hsph.harvard.edu/nutritionsource/omega-3-fats/

Exercise

Association for Psychological Science. (2013, October 21). Learning New Skills Keeps an Aging Mind Sharp. Retrieved from https://www.psychologicalscience.org/news/releases/learning-new-skills-keeps-an-aging-mind-sharp.html

Bak, T. H., Nissan, J. J., Allerhand, M. M., & Deary, I. J. (2014, June 02). Does bilingualism influence cognitive aging? Retrieved from http://onlinelibrary.wiley.com/doi/10.1002/ana.24158/full

BBC. (2017, April 25). Exercise 'keeps the mind sharp' in over-50s, study finds. Retrieved from http://www.bbc.com/news/health-39693462

Blue, A. (2014, May 2). What Our Ancestors Can Teach Us About Exercise, Alzheimer's and Human Longevity. Retrieved from https://uanews.arizona.edu/story/what-our-ancestors-can-teach-us-about-exercise-alzheimer-s-and-human-longevity

Gómez-Pinilla, F. (2008, July). Brain foods: the effects of nutrients on brain function. Retrieved December 13, 2017, from https://www.ncbi.nlm.nih.gov/pmc/articles/PMC2805706/

Indivero, V. M. (2014, November 12). Learning languages is a workout for brains, both young and old. Retrieved from http://news.psu.edu/story/334349/2014/11/12/research/learning-languages-workout-brains-both-young-and-old

Nacamulli, M., Labovic, B., LaBracio, L., Gendler, A., & Chen, P. (2015, June 23). The benefits of a bilingual brain . Retrieved from https://ed.ted.com/lessons/how-speaking-multiple-languages-benefits-the-brain-mia-nacamulli YouTUbe Link: https://www.youtube.com/watch?v=MMmOLN5zBLY

Sleep

Alhola, P. & Polo-Kantola, P. (2007). Sleep deprivation: Impact on cognitive performance. Neuropsychiatric Disease and Treatment, 3(5), 553–567.
Retrieved from
https://www.ncbi.nlm.nih.gov/pmc/articles/PMC2656292/

Beccuti, G., & Pannain, S. (2011, July). Sleep and obesity. Retrieved from
https://www.ncbi.nlm.nih.gov/pmc/articles/PMC3632337/

Boult, A. (2017, May 26). Sleep deprivation can cause brain to start 'eating' itself. Retrieved from
http://www.telegraph.co.uk/science/2017/05/26/sleep-deprivation-can-cause-brain-start-eating/

Edinger, J., Manber, R., Krystal, A., & Buysse, D. (2017, April 28). 0335 Does Objective sleep duration moderate treatment response in patient with comorbid depression and insomnia? A report from the triad study| Sleep | Oxford Academic. Retrieved from https://academic.oup.com/sleep/article-abstract/40/suppl_1/A124/3781583?redirectedFrom=fulltext

Harvard Medical School. (2007, December 18). Natural Patterns of Sleep. Retrieved from http://healthysleep.med.harvard.edu/healthy/science/what/sleep-patterns-rem-nrem

Hun, K., & Ng, N. (2015, January 19). Man dies after 3-day Internet gaming binge. Retrieved from http://edition.cnn.com/2015/01/19/world/taiwan-gamer-death/index.html

McNamara, P., Auerbach, S., Johnson, P., Harris, E., & Doros, G. (2010, May). Impact of REM sleep on distortions of self-concept, mood and memory in depressed/anxious participants. Retrieved from https://www.ncbi.nlm.nih.gov/pmc/articles/PMC2847051/

PBS Nova. (2012, September 30). What Are Dreams. Retrieved from https://vimeo.com/50488042

World Science Festival. (2015, March 18). The Mind After Midnight: Where Do You Go When You Go to Sleep? Retrieved from https://www.youtube.com/watch?v=stXhGMVJuqA

Part 4 : Developing Intuition

Chapter 5   Thinking Methods

Timing is everything

Holman, C., & Villers-Sidani, E. D. (2014, April 11). Indestructible plastic: the neuroscience of the new aging brain. Retrieved from https://www.ncbi.nlm.nih.gov/pmc/articles/PMC3990104/

Holz, J., Piosczyk, H., Landmann, N., Feige, B., Spiegelhalder, K., Riemann, D., Voderholzer, U. (2012, July 12). The Timing of Learning before Night-Time Sleep Differentially Affects Declarative and Procedural Long-Term Memory Consolidation in Adolescents. Retrieved from http://journals.plos.org/plosone/article?id=10.1371%2Fjournal.pone.0040963

Memory and Imagination

The right way to worry

The Tri-unity Approach

Positive + Negative = Workable Area

Past + Future = Present

Triple Perspective = Me + S/He/Them = Us

Multidirectional Thinking

Understanding and Appreciation

Philippine Statistics Authority. (2015). 2015 Philippine Statistical Yearbook [Pdf]. Retrieved from https://psa.gov.ph/sites/default/files/2015%20PSY%20PDF.pdf   ISSN 0118-1564

The Centre

Removing the Blinders

Merriam-Webster. (2017, November 20). Blinder. Retrieved from https://www.merriam-webster.com/dictionary/blinder

Peripheral Vision and the Sidelights

Cambridge Dictionary. (n.d.). Sidelight Meaning in the Cambridge English Dictionary. Retrieved from https://dictionary.cambridge.org/dictionary/english/sidelight

Dictionary.com Unabridged (n.d.). Peripheral vision. Retrieved from Dictionary.com website http://www.dictionary.com/browse/peripheral-vision

Dictionary.com Unabridged (n.d.). Sidelight. Retrieved from Dictionary.com website http://www.dictionary.com/browse/sidelight?s=t

Chapter 6   Intuition tools

Diary or Journal

Murnahan, B. (2012, February 20). Stress and Anxiety Reduction Due to Writing Diaries, Journals, E-mail, and Weblogs. Retrieved from http://commons.emich.edu/honors/230/

Frequencies and Entrainment

Brainworksneurotherapy.com. (n.d.). What are Brainwaves? Retrieved from http://www.brainworksneurotherapy.com/what-are-brainwaves

Chaieb, L., Wilpert, E. C., Reber, T. P., & Fell, J. (2015, May 12). Auditory Beat Stimulation and its Effects on Cognition and Mood States. Retrieved from https://www.ncbi.nlm.nih.gov/pmc/articles/PMC4428073/

Brain Waves

Ammanuel, S., Chan, W. C., Adler, D. A., Lakshamanan, B. M., Gupta, S. S., Ewen, J. B., Kadam, S. D. (2015, October 7). Heightened Delta Power during Slow-Wave-Sleep in Patients with Rett Syndrome Associated with Poor Sleep Efficiency. Retrieved from https://www.ncbi.nlm.nih.gov/pmc/articles/PMC4596813/

Brugnoli, M. P., Brugnoli, A., & Recchia, L. (2016). A new Classification of the Modified States of Consciousness. La Lambert Academic Publishing ISBN 9783659856839. Retrieved from https://www.researchgate.net/profile/Maria_Brugnoli2/publicat ion/306381049_A_new_classification_of_the_modified_states_ of_consciousness_A_peer-reviewed_referenced_resource/links/57bc3e3408ae51eef1f617 b3/A-new-classification-of-the-modified-states-of-consciousness-A-peer-reviewed-referenced-resource.pdf

Budzynski, T., PhD. (1992). The Clinical Guide to Sound and Light [Pdf]. Tools for Exploration. Retrieved from https://web.stanford.edu/group/brainwaves/2006/theclinicalgu idetosoundandlight.pdf

Chen, Z., Cao, J., Cao, Y., Zhang, Y., Gu, F., Zhu, G., Cichocki, A. (2008, April 19). An empirical EEG analysis in brain death diagnosis for adults. Retrieved from https://www.ncbi.nlm.nih.gov/pmc/articles/PMC2518749/

Fink, A., & Benedek, M. (2012, December 12). EEG alpha power and creative ideation. Retrieved from http://www.sciencedirect.com/science/article/pii/S0149763412 002114 https://doi.org/10.1016/j.neubiorev.2012.12.002

Groppe, D. M., Bickel, S., Keller, C. J., Jain, S. K., Hwang, S. T., Harden, C., & Mehta, A. D. (2013, October 01). Dominant frequencies of resting human brain activity as measured by the electrocorticogram. Retrieved from https://www.ncbi.nlm.nih.gov/pmc/articles/PMC4269223/

Hall, R. (1998). Stages of Sleep. Retrieved from https://web.mst.edu/~psyworld/sleep_stages.htm

Herrman, N. (n.d.). What is the function of the various brainwaves? Retrieved from https://www.scientificamerican.com/article/what-is-the-function-of-t-1997-12-22/

Lutz, A., Greischar, L. L., Rawlings, N. B., Ricard, M., & Davidson, R. J. (2004, November 16). Long-term meditators self-induce high-amplitude gamma synchrony during mental practice. Retrieved from http://www.pnas.org/content/101/46/16369.long

Millet, D. (2002, June 3). The origins of EEG. Retrieved from http://www.bri.ucla.edu/nha/ishn/ab24-2002.htm

Roth, T. (2009). Slow Wave Sleep: Does it Matter? Journal of Clinical Sleep Medicine : JCSM : Official Publication of the American Academy of Sleep Medicine, 5(2 Suppl), S4–S5.
Retrieved from https://www.ncbi.nlm.nih.gov/pmc/articles/PMC2824210/

Sousa, A. D. (2013, April 30). Towards An Integrative Theory Of Consciousness: Part 1 (Neurobiological And Cognitive Models). Retrieved from https://www.ncbi.nlm.nih.gov/pmc/articles/PMC3653219/

Westminster College. (n.d.). The Measurement of Brain Waves. Retrieved from
http://www.psych.westminster.edu/psybio/BN/Labs/Brainwaves.htm

Winerman, L. (2005, January). Imaginary friends last into the school-age years. Retrieved from
http://www.apa.org/monitor/jan05/imaginary.aspx

Brain Entrainment

Budzynski, T., PhD. (1992). The Clinical Guide to Sound and Light [Pdf]. Tools for Exploration. Retrieved from
https://web.stanford.edu/group/brainwaves/2006/theclinicalguidetosoundandlight.pdf

Chaieb, L., Wilpert, E. C., Reber, T. P., & Fell, J. (2015, May 12). Auditory Beat Stimulation and its Effects on Cognition and Mood States. Retrieved from
https://www.ncbi.nlm.nih.gov/pmc/articles/PMC4428073/

Warburton, M. (2015, September 29). Hack Your Mind: Understanding Brainwave Frequencies. Retrieved from
http://fractalpanda.com/hack-your-mind-understanding-brainwave-frequencies/

Nature

Meditation

Hernández, S. E., Suero, J., Barros, A., González-Mora, J. L., & Rubia, K. (2016, March 3). Increased Grey Matter Associated with Long-Term Sahaja Yoga Meditation: A Voxel-Based Morphometry Study. Retrieved from
http://journals.plos.org/plosone/article?id=10.1371%2Fjournal.pone.0150757

Hölzel, B. K., Carmody, J., Vangel, M., Congleton, C., Yerramsetti, S. M., Gard, T., & Lazar, S. W. (2010, November 10). Mindfulness practice leads to increases in regional brain gray matter density. Retrieved from https://www.ncbi.nlm.nih.gov/pmc/articles/PMC3004979/

Dreams

Markov, D., Jaffe, F., & Doghramji, K. (2006, July). Update on Parasomnias: A Review for Psychiatric Practice. Retrieved from https://www.ncbi.nlm.nih.gov/pmc/articles/PMC2958868/

PBS Nova. (2012, September 30). What Are Dreams. Retrieved from https://vimeo.com/50488042

Lucid Dreaming

Dream Interpretation

Tarot

The Deck

Reflection

Part 5 : Fantastical Intuition

Chapter 7   Back to the Beginning

Dougherty, E. (2011, April 26). What are thoughts made of? Retrieved from https://engineering.mit.edu/engage/ask-an-engineer/what-are-thoughts-made-of/

J., T. (2007, October 22). Q & A: Car traveling at the speed of light? Retrieved from https://van.physics.illinois.edu/qa/listing.php?id=1355

Acknowledgements

I'd like to thank those who generously gave their time, encouragement, and support while I wrote this book and towards the finishing touches.

To my ever wonderful and generous husband, Andy Henkel, you are my inspiration, my rock, and my number one fan. Thank you for your patience (especially when I forced you to listen to what I'd written every time I finished a chapter, and to read the whole book when done, ha ha ha!), love and support, which were vital in making this book — a labour of love — happen.

To Alana Marie Garrigues, my line editor, thanks for your thoroughness, eye for detail, hard work, patience and of course, clear and prompt communication, and for making my book shine!

To Nathaniel Dasco, my book designer, thanks for getting me — my vision for the book cover — and translating it into a beautiful design that truly resonates with me.

To Dr Sharon Schembri, thank you for lending me your keen eyes, brilliant mind, and enthusiasm in ever-so-promptly giving me your valuable feedback.

To Gary Mclean, thanks for being game in reading your first book on intuition. I'm so glad it was my book, and I'm pleased to know it didn't traumatise you. Kidding aside, I hope you found it interesting. Cheers!

To Mark Ascroft, thanks for your encouragement, pointers, and enjoyable discussions over coffee.

To Steve Bell, thanks for your authentic and interesting perspective.

To Rommel Carrera, thank you for your insightful suggestions.

And to Jack Hall, thank you for your kindness and generosity.